Oxford School *Shakespeare*

MACBETH

edited by
Roma Gill, OBE
M.A. *Cantab.*, B. Litt. *Oxon*

OXFORD
UNIVERSITY PRESS

OXFORD

UNIVERSITY PRESS

Great Clarendon Street, Oxford OX2 6DP

Oxford University Press is a department of the University of Oxford.
It furthers the University's objective of excellence in research, scholarship, and
education by publishing worldwide in

Oxford New York

Athens Auckland Bangkok Bogotá Buenos Aires Cape Town Chennai
Dar es Salaam Delhi Florence Hong Kong Istanbul Karachi Kolkata
Kuala Lumpur Madrid Melbourne Mexico City Mumbai Nairobi Paris
São Paulo Shanghai Singapore Taipei Tokyo Toronto Warsaw

with associated companies in Berlin Ibadan

OXFORD is a registered trade mark of Oxford University Press
in the UK and in certain other countries

ISBN 0 19 832022 1 (Schools edition) 3 5 7 9 10 8 6 4
ISBN 0 19 832023 X (Trade edition) 3 5 7 9 10 8 6 4

Illustrations by Alexy Pendle

Cover photograph by Robbie Jack/Corbis shows Hilary Lyon as Lady Macbeth
and Paul Higgins as Macbeth in the Lyric, Hammersmith 1996 production of
Macbeth. Inside photographs are by Donald Cooper (Photostage).

For Mandy

Oxford School Shakespeare
edited by Roma Gill

Typeset by Herb Bowes Graphics, Oxford
Printed by Alden Group, Oxford

Contents

Introduction

About the Play

When Elizabeth I of England was dying, childless, she named James VI of Scotland as her successor. He became James I of England.

In August 1606 James was at Hampton Court, a palace near London, entertaining his brother-in-law, King Christian of Denmark. A play was acted for them, *Macbeth*, written by the best dramatist of the time, William Shakespeare. It was a new play, but the story was an old one, and James knew it well, because it was about the ancestors, Banquo and Fleance, through whom he had inherited the throne of Scotland.

Shakespeare found the story in *The History of Scotland*, by Raphael Holinshed, but his play is much more than a dramatic re-writing of the historical facts. He made many changes, and the biggest of these concerned James's ancestor. In the true story, Banquo joined Macbeth in killing Duncan; but clearly it would be tactless to suggest that James was descended from a regicide—the murderer of a king. So Shakespeare's Banquo is innocent.

James also believed that he was descended spiritually from the long tradition of English monarchs, and that he had inherited the power of healing that Edward the Confessor (1042–66) possessed. Shakespeare's description of this power (4, 3, 148–58) is, to some extent, deliberate flattery of his king. Shakespeare also knew that James was extremely interested in witchcraft and had written a book about it.

Macbeth is certainly a play 'fit for a king'.

But of course it is more than this—more than flattery for an ancient British monarch; and although the story is largely true, we do not read *Macbeth* as 'history'. We could interpret Shakespeare's play as a moral lesson. Macbeth murders his king. To murder any man is a crime, but those who lived at the time of Shakespeare thought that the murder of a *king* was the greatest of all crimes. Kings were appointed by God, to rule as His deputies: rebellion against a true king was rebellion against God. By murdering Duncan, Macbeth gains the crown; but he loses love, friendship, respect—and in the end his life. His crime is rightly punished.

There is still more to the play. On one 'level' it is royal entertainment—and entertainment, too, for all those of us who enjoy the suspense and excitement of a murder story. On another level, it teaches us, in a new way, the old lesson that crime does not pay. But there are at least two more levels.

As we look at the character of Macbeth we see, more clearly than we are able to see in real life, the effects of uncontrolled ambition on a man who is, except for his ambition, noble in nature. Macbeth has full knowledge of right and wrong; he knows that he has committed a very great crime by murdering Duncan. Shakespeare shows us how Macbeth becomes hardened to his crimes, and yet how he suffers from fears which he has created himself.

On another level, the play has great power as a work of poetry and imagination. The language is rich in sound and meaning, full of pictures, and immensely varied. Take this episode, for example. When Macbeth comes from the murder of Duncan, his hands are covered in the king's blood; he looks at them, and feels that all the waters in the ocean cannot wash away the blood, but that

> this my hand will rather
> The multitudinous seas incarnadine,
> Making the green one red.   (2, 2, 64–6)

The word 'multitudinous' gives a sense of vastness, and 'incarnadine' (meaning 'redden') is another impressive word; its length and sound give strength to the meaning. The two words are more Latin than English, and were very new to the English language; Shakespeare was one of the first writers to use them. They are followed by the simplest, most direct words. Imagine a film camera. First the camera shows you a picture of endless waters, stretching as far as the eye can see: then a sudden close-up picture, perhaps a small pool of green water that turns red with blood as we look at it. Such skill in the use of language is unique.

Although I have distinguished four levels on which the play *Macbeth* can work, I do not want to give the impression that these levels can in fact be separated from each other. The entertainment, the moral teaching, the psychology, and the poetry are often all contained in the same speech—even, sometimes, in the same line. *Macbeth* demands an alert reader.

No summary can do justice to the play. At best, a commentary such as the one here can be no more than a map. It can show the roads, and even point out the important places; but it is no substitute for reading the play.

Leading Characters in the Play

Duncan The King of Scotland (*c.* 1034); he is presented as a true and gracious monarch—the embodiment of the Elizabethan notion that a king was appointed as God's deputy on earth and was himself almost divine.

Malcolm Duncan's elder son. Early in the play Malcolm is named as the next king of Scotland—and consequently he becomes the prime suspect when Duncan is murdered.

Macbeth A mighty and ambitious warrior, one of the leaders of Duncan's army. A witches' prophecy leads him to murder Duncan so that he himself can be king—but his conscience afterwards will never let him rest.

Lady Macbeth She is even more ambitious than her husband, and has fewer moral scruples. She urges Macbeth to kill Duncan, and refuses to understand his doubts and hesitations. Gradually her close relationship with Macbeth crumbles into nothing.

Banquo Macbeth's co-commander in Duncan's army; he also hears the witches' prophecies, but resists their temptation.

Macduff A Scottish thane (= nobleman) who comes to prominence after the murder of Duncan and leads the opposition to Macbeth.

Ross A valuable commentator on the action of the play and its effects in the wider world outside Macbeth's castle.

The Witches These supernatural phenomena, called the 'weird sisters' in Shakespeare's historical source-book, are related to the three Fates in classical mythology. Productions have represented them variously as grotesque and frightening, comic and ridiculous; young and beautiful; masked and hideous.

Synopsis

Act 1

Act 2

ACT 3

SCENE 1   Banquo is suspicious—and Macbeth arranges to have him murdered by two hired assassins.

SCENE 2   Lady Macbeth is uneasy: Macbeth assures her that everything is under control, but he refuses to tell her what he is planning.

SCENE 3   The murder of Banquo—but Fleance escapes from the murderers.

SCENE 4   Macbeth and his wife welcome the guests to their state banquet. The Ghost of Banquo appears but only Macbeth can see it, and his strange behaviour startles Lady Macbeth and their guests.

SCENE 5   The witches and their queen Hecate prepare the audience for the next meeting with Macbeth.

SCENE 6   Lennox and an unnamed Lord discuss the state of affairs: Malcolm is in England, Macduff has gone to join him, and the English king is raising an army to fight against Macbeth.

ACT 4

SCENE 1   The witches assemble to meet Macbeth, and promise to answer his questions. Their magic Apparitions comfort him at first—and then give cause for alarm.

SCENE 2   Lady Macduff questions Ross about her husband's flight, and then tries to explain the situation to her little son. A Messenger warns her to flee from the palace, but it is too late and the murderers rush into the room.

SCENE 3   Macduff has joined Malcolm at the court of Edward the Confessor, and the two men, at first suspicious of each other, test their loyalties. Plans are in hand for an invasion of Scotland by the English king—but then Macduff hears of the murder of his wife and children.

ACT 5

SCENE 1   Lady Macbeth suffers from a guilty conscience. She walks in her sleep, and dreams that she and her husband are murdering King Duncan.

SCENE 2   A section of the army marches towards Dunsinane, and their leaders discuss the enemy, Macbeth, who is showing signs of panic.

Scene 3   When he is told of the approaching armies, Macbeth tries to comfort himself by recalling the witches' prophecies. He discusses his wife's condition with the Doctor, then goes off to do battle.

Scene 4   Malcolm's soldiers camouflage themselves with branches from the trees of Birnam Wood.

Scene 5   The battle is at its height when Seyton brings news to Macbeth that his wife has just died—and a Messenger tells him that Birnam Wood is moving towards Dunsinane.

Scene 6   Malcolm's army reaches Macbeth's castle: battle is commenced.

Scene 7   Macbeth encounters Young Siward and kills him; Macduff comes in search of Macbeth, they fight, and Macbeth is killed. Malcolm is proclaimed King.

Macbeth: commentary

SCENE 1　A very short scene opens the play. It is long enough to awaken curiosity, but not to satisfy it. We have come in at the *end* of the witches' meeting, just as they are arranging their next appointment before their 'familiar spirits'—devils in animal shapes—call them away into the 'fog and filthy air'. The mood of the play is set here, although the action does not

SCENE 2　start until the next scene. Here we learn about the tough battle, about the rebels who seem to have all the luck, and about two brave men, Macbeth and Banquo, who win the victory for Scotland. Duncan rewards Macbeth for his courage by giving him the title 'thane of Cawdor'; but we ought to remember that the title first belonged to one who was 'a most disloyal traitor'.

SCENE 3　The witches' malice and magic are shown, as they await Macbeth on the lonely moor (a wasteland area). They have power over the winds, and can make life miserable for such men as the captain of the ship, 'The Tiger'. Their dance, when they hear Macbeth's drum, is made up of steps in groups of three—the magical number. Macbeth and Banquo, however, are ordinary human beings, tired after the day's fighting and grumbling about the weather. Banquo is almost amused by the witches; he cannot bring himself to think of them as women because 'your beards forbid me to interpret | That you are so'. Macbeth is stunned to silence by their prophecies, but Banquo questions them calmly.

　　The audience can judge the witches better than Macbeth can; *we* know, from the previous scene, that his courage, and not the witches' magic, has won him the title 'thane of Cawdor'; and we are not surprised, as he is, when Ross calls him by this title. While Ross, Angus, and Banquo speak together (perhaps at the back of the stage), Macbeth speaks his own thoughts aloud in a soliloquy—a speech not intended by the speaker to be overheard. They are frightening thoughts: they frighten Macbeth as well as us, for murder is in his mind. He tries to reject this first impulse, declaring that he will leave everything to chance:

> If chance will have me king, why chance may crown me
> Without my stir.

SCENE 4   When Duncan hears of the death of the treacherous thane of Cawdor, he utters a very meaningful remark:

> There's no art
> To find the mind's construction in the face.
> He was a gentleman on whom I built
> An absolute trust.

We have not seen the traitor, so we do not know how appropriate these words are for *him*; but we have seen his successor, and Macbeth is certainly a gentleman on whom Duncan is building 'An absolute trust'. Duncan's comment could also be applied to other persons and happenings in this play, where things are not what they seem to be, where 'Fair is foul and foul is fair'.

Duncan now makes a very important announcement:

> We will establish our estate upon
> Our eldest, Malcolm, whom we name hereafter
> The Prince of Cumberland.

In the time of Duncan the crown of Scotland was not passed automatically from father to son. Instead, the king could name his successor, as Duncan does here, and grant him the title 'Prince of Cumberland'. If the king were to die without naming an heir, or if the heir was not acceptable, the Scottish nobles could elect a new king. We hear that Macbeth is thus elected in *Act 2*, Scene 4. Duncan's choice comes as a great shock to Macbeth, for he recognizes it as an obstacle standing between him and the crown. At the end of the scene he admits to possessing 'black and deep desires', but he is afraid to speak these openly, even to himself.

SCENE 5   We already know the contents of Macbeth's letter to his wife; but the letter is important because it shows us something of the relationship between Macbeth and Lady Macbeth: he has no secrets from her, and she is his 'dearest partner of greatness'. Lady Macbeth understands her husband well. She knows that he has great ambitions, but she also knows that he is honourable, and that this sense of honour will not allow him to 'catch the nearest way'. She knows that she will have to urge her husband on to become king, and she calls for evil spirits to help her. She will give up all the gentle, tender qualities of a woman, so that she can become a sexless, pitiless fiend. She takes full control over the situation, and Macbeth seems glad to let her have the responsibility.

SCENE 6   Duncan and his followers appreciate the peaceful harmony of Macbeth's castle, where Lady Macbeth welcomes the guests with an overflow of polite compliments—which even the audience can barely understand.

SCENE 7   Alone after dinner, Macbeth has an opportunity to think about the murder of his king, perhaps for the first time. At first murder had been only a dream, 'but fantastical' (1, 3, 138), but now it is a real moral problem. He knows that the crime must be punished; divine justice in a 'life to come' does not worry him so much as judgement in this earthly life. Then he considers the duties he owes to Duncan—the duties of a kinsman, of a subject to his king, and of a host to his guest. Finally he thinks of the character of Duncan, a king of almost divine excellence.

Macbeth has a vision of the heavenly powers, horrified by this murder; he sees Pity personified as a 'naked new-born babe' which is nevertheless 'Striding the blast', while 'heaven's cherubin' are mounted on the winds. The speech builds to a mighty climax—then suddenly the power is lost, when Macbeth turns to his own wretched motive for committing such a crime. He can find nothing except 'Vaulting ambition', and even now he realizes that too high a leap ('vault') can only lead to a fall.

His mind is made up, and he tells his wife 'We will proceed no further in this business'. He is not prepared for her rage and abuse. She calls him a coward, insults his virility, and declares that she would have murdered her child while it was feeding at her breast, rather than break such a promise as Macbeth has done. Defeated by his wife's scorn, and persuaded by her encouragement, Macbeth agrees to murder his king.

ACT 2

SCENE 1   The witches have disturbed Banquo, as well as Macbeth. As he crosses the courtyard of Macbeth's castle he hears a noise, and calls for his sword: this suggests tension, for he should not need a sword in a friend's home. Macbeth also shows signs of stress, for he speaks few words in his replies to Banquo; and when he is alone, the strain shows very clearly. He is living in a nightmare, but although he is at first alarmed by the dagger that his imagination creates, he seems later to *enjoy* the horror of the moment. The last lines of the scene could even show a grim humour:

the bell invites me.

Hear it not, Duncan, for it is a knell

That summons thee to heaven or to hell.

SCENE 2   Lady Macbeth is as tense as her husband, and she has been drinking to give herself courage. Her speech is jerky, for she reacts to every sound, and when her husband comes from the king's room, his hands red with Duncan's blood, she greets him with relief and pride: 'My husband'. He has now proved himself, in her eyes, to be a man. Macbeth slowly awakens from the nightmare he has been living in and realizes what a terrible crime he has committed. He speaks of the real sounds he has heard, and then of the voice that cried

'Sleep no more:

Macbeth does murder sleep'

This ban will be carried out: never again will Macbeth, or his wife, have any rest, and from time to time throughout the play they will comment on their weariness and lack of refreshing sleep.

For the present, however, Lady Macbeth again takes charge of the situation. Early in this scene she revealed some natural, womanly feelings when she confessed that she could not murder Duncan herself because he 'resembled | My father as he slept'. But now she speaks a line which shows, terrifyingly, how little she thinks of the guilt that she shares with her husband:

A little water clears us of this deed.

SCENE 3   The mood of the play suddenly changes. The audience has been as tense as Macbeth and Lady Macbeth in the last scene, and we need to relax a little now. The Porter, woken from a drunken sleep, gives us something to laugh at. His jokes are not so funny today as they were in 1606, when his chatter about the 'equivocator' might have reminded the audience of the recent and notorious trial of a priest who could 'swear in both the scales against either scale'; but the wise observations on drink and lechery are still amusing.

Macduff and Lennox come almost from another world; or perhaps the Porter is more accurate than he thinks when he pretends to be porter at the gate of hell. The tension mounts again as we wait for the murder to be discovered.

Lennox's description of the 'unruly' night would have been full of significance to the Elizabethans. They firmly believed that any disorder in human affairs was reflected by disorder in the world of nature.

Macbeth is cautious, but we cannot miss the understatement of his reply to Lennox: ''twas a rough night'.

The moment we have been waiting for arrives. Macduff's words emphasize the fact that this is more than an ordinary murder:

> Confusion now hath made his masterpiece:
> Most sacrilegious murder hath broke ope
> The Lord's anointed temple.

The scene is chaotic: alarm-bells ring, and characters appear from all sides of the stage. Macduff is almost hysterical; the king's sons are afraid; Macbeth impulsively kills Duncan's servants—and by doing so arouses Macduff's suspicion. The speech in which Macbeth attempts to justify himself may perhaps convince the other thanes; but we know how false it is, and the elaborate images ('His silver skin lac'd with his golden blood') stress this falsehood. Lady Macbeth knows the truth too, for she faints (or pretends to faint) and some attention is drawn away from her husband.

SCENE 4   The short scene between Ross and the Old Man serves three purposes. At first it continues the comparison begun in Lennox's lines in Scene 3 between the human world and the natural world, mentioning strange events and stressing that they are

>   unnatural,
> Even like the deed that's done.

The second function of the scene appears when Macduff enters to bring more news: it indicates the passing of time. Thirdly, it brings Macduff into greater prominence, because it allows the actor to reveal, by the tone of his voice, that Macduff continues to be suspicious of Macbeth, and that he does not himself believe the answers he gives to Ross's questions.

ACT 3

SCENE 1   Banquo also is suspicious of Macbeth:

> Thou hast it now, King, Cawdor, Glamis, all,
> As the weïrd women promis'd, and I fear
> Thou played'st most foully for't

But he thinks about the prophecy concerning his own children, and this gives him hope. Macbeth too has been thinking about this prophecy, and it gives him cause for bitterness: he realizes that his crown is 'fruitless', and his sceptre 'barren'. He murdered Duncan in order to make the witches' prophecy come true, but now he plots to murder Banquo and Fleance so that the witches' promise to Banquo may *not* come true.

SCENE 2   Lady Macbeth now begins to show signs of strain, and we hear that Macbeth suffers 'terrible dreams'. For a moment Macbeth and his wife show understanding and sympathy for each other, but the moment does not last long. Macbeth keeps secret from his wife the plot to murder Banquo. He alarms her by conjuring up an atmosphere of evil, and once again he appears to enjoy his dreadful imaginings (just as he did when he went to murder Duncan). But it is a mistake to hide the facts from Lady Macbeth: this is the beginning of the break in their relationship.

When Macbeth calls upon 'seeling night' to hide his wickedness, we remember how Lady Macbeth, before the murder of Duncan, had called for the night, shrouded in 'the dunnest smoke of hell' (1, 5, 50), to hide the murdering dagger from the sight of heaven.

SCENE 3   Outside the castle, the two murderers wait for Banquo and Fleance. It is a surprise, to us as well as to them, when a third hired assassin appears. Macbeth can trust no one, not even the thugs he first appointed to murder Banquo.

SCENE 4   The confusion of Banquo's murder contrasts well with the ceremony of the state banquet. The formality is announced in the first line: 'You know your own degrees; sit down'; and the scene proceeds with dignity for some time. The appearance of one of Banquo's murderers disturbs the peace for Macbeth. The state occasion demands courteous behaviour from the king, but when the murderer says that Fleance has escaped, Macbeth is agitated. Banquo's Ghost, which only Macbeth can see, adds to this distress, until the whole scene breaks into fragments, and Lady Macbeth has to ask her guests to leave, without any of the formality with which they arrived:

> Stand not upon the order of your going,
> But go at once.

The banquet is symbolic as well as realistic, and Shakespeare is careful that we do not overlook this aspect. As soon as the guests are seated, Macbeth promises to 'drink a measure | The table round'. In many societies and religions, the sharing of a cup of wine, sometimes even called a 'loving-cup', symbolizes unity and fellowship; and so it is intended here. When Macbeth has stepped away from the table to speak to the murderer, Lady Macbeth calls him back, and reminds him of his duty as a host, adding that on such an occasion 'the sauce to meat is ceremony'. Macbeth brings chaos to Scotland, breaking up the harmony of a well-ordered country, just as he breaks up the state banquet 'With most admir'd disorder'.

SCENE 5   It is a pity that this silly little scene has to be included in *Macbeth*. Shakespeare never wrote like this, and it was probably inserted into the play by some over-enthusiastic actor, who saw that the audiences enjoyed the witches' scenes, and decided to give them another!

SCENE 6   Suspicion of Macbeth is growing. Lennox speaks here not as himself, an individual character, but with what we now call 'the voice of the people'. His words are innocent in meaning, but the exaggeration of tone directs the actor to make his speech heavily sarcastic—for example in:

> How it did grieve Macbeth! Did he not straight
> In pious rage the two delinquents tear,
> That were the slaves of drink and thralls of sleep?

The unnamed Lord gives us information about Malcolm, and also makes the first reference in the play to the king of England, 'the most pious Edward', who is the complete opposite of Macbeth. The comparison will be developed in a later scene.

ACT 4

SCENE 1   We now see Macbeth receiving comfort from the three Apparitions that the witches call up. They appear in symbolic form. The first, 'an armed head', represents Macbeth's own head (wearing a helmet); the 'bloody child' that comes next is Macduff, who had been 'untimely ripp'd' from his mother's womb (as he tells Macbeth in *Act* 5, Scene 7); and the last, the royal child with a tree in his hand, is Malcolm, the rightful king of Scotland, who approaches the palace at Dunsinane camouflaged with tree-branches (*Act* 5, Scene 4). Macbeth cannot interpret these symbols, but Shakespeare expects the audience to understand what is meant. This is 'dramatic irony'—when the truth of a situation is known to the audience but hidden from the characters in the play. There is dramatic irony, too, in the words spoken by the Apparitions, for again we understand the real meanings, while Macbeth can only understand the apparent meanings of the words. Macbeth, however, is in no doubt about the significance of the final 'show of Eight Kings'.

SCENE 2   This pathetic scene in which Lady Macduff and her son are massacred shows us Macbeth's cruelty in action. When he plotted to kill Banquo's son, Fleance, he could justify the crime to himself by referring to the prophecy that Banquo's children should be kings. But he is in no danger from Lady Macduff or from her son, and the crime is more dreadful because it is motiveless. Our knowledge of it helps us to find more

SCENE 3   dramatic irony in the scene that follows, when Malcolm mistrusts Macduff chiefly because he cannot understand

> Why in that rawness left you wife and child,
> Those precious motives, those strong knots of love,
> Without leave-taking?

Macduff must prove his loyalty to Malcolm and to Scotland; then Malcolm must prove that he is worthy to be king. Again we are told of Edward the Confessor, and this time we hear of his divine gift of healing. This characteristic was not chosen by chance. Shakespeare uses many images of sickness; just a little later in this scene, he describes Scotland as a place where

> good men's lives
> Expire before the flowers in their caps,
> Dying or ere they sicken.

In *Act 5*, Scene 2 Caithness recognizes Malcolm as the doctor who can cure Scotland's sickness, calling him 'the med'cine of the sickly weal' (line 27).

We respond intellectually to this account of the English king, and to the concept of the monarch as some kind of physician, divinely appointed to safeguard the country's health. We respond emotionally to the next episode in this long scene as Ross breaks the bad news to Macduff. We feel the painful irony of Ross's evasive answer: 'they were well at peace when I did leave 'em'. If we had not seen Lady Macduff and her son, we should not be distressed; because of Scene 2, we are able to share Macduff's own grief. I am always moved by Macduff's answer to Malcolm, who urges him to

> Dispute it like a man.

Macduff replies with dignity

> I shall do so;
> But I must also feel it as a man.

The word 'man' is being used in two senses. Malcolm intends it to mean 'bravely', but Macduff is thinking of a man as a human being, with tender emotions of love and grief, which must not be denied.

ACT 5

SCENE 1   The very next scene shows what happens when human emotions are denied. At the beginning of the play Lady Macbeth prayed that she should know 'no compunctious visitings of nature' (1, 5, 44) that might prevent her from murdering Duncan. Now she walks in her sleep, and her mind constantly re-lives the night of the murder. On that night she declared confidently that 'A little water clears us of this deed' (2, 2, 70), but now she knows that 'all the perfumes of Arabia will not sweeten this little hand'. It is the last time we see Lady Macbeth. Although the Doctor warns her lady-in-waiting to 'Remove from her the means of all annoyance', we learn later that 'by self and violent hands', she killed herself (5, 9, 37).

SCENE 2   From now until the end of the play the action moves between the two armies—Malcolm's soldiers, steadily drawing closer to Dunsinane, and Macbeth's forces, besieged near the castle. Caithness and Angus discuss the strength of the enemy, and Angus offers a shrewd comment on Macbeth:

> Now does he feel his title
> Hang loose about him, like a giant's robe
> Upon a dwarfish thief.

This is not the first image of badly-fitting clothes. When Macbeth was given the title 'thane of Cawdor', soon after the witches had prophesied that it would be given to him, he stood apart from Banquo and the king's messengers; Banquo laughed, and explained that Macbeth was like a man with new clothes:

> New honours come upon him
> Like our strange garments, cleave not to their mould,
> But with the aid of use.   (1, 3, 143–5)

Macbeth himself thought of the praises he had earned for his courage in terms of fine clothes,

> Which would be worn now in their newest gloss,
> Not cast aside so soon.   (1, 7, 34–5)

There are many such allusions throughout the play. They make us stop and think about the relationship between Macbeth and the honours he is 'wearing'. Has he won them, or stolen them? Will his 'clothes' fit, in time—or will they always be too big for him?

SCENE 3   When he has heard the Doctor's medical opinion of his wife, Macbeth asks, with his grim humour, for a medical opinion on the state of the country. The Doctor is allowed the same humour when he closes the scene:

> Were I from Dunsinane away and clear,
> Profit again should hardly draw me here.

The situation is now so serious that only a sour joke (playing on the generally accepted belief that doctors are greedy for gold) can ease the tension.

SCENE 4   Birnam Wood begins to move; what seemed like witches' magic is seen to be elementary military tactics. Excitement and tension mount, as the
SCENE 5   soldiers come closer to Dunsinane. But Macbeth does not respond to the excitement: he has lost the capacity for feeling either fear or, as we see when he hears of his wife's death, grief. He speaks the most disillusioned words that Shakespeare ever wrote when he contemplates life and its 'petty pace from day to day'. He still hopes that the witches' promises (made to him in *Act 4*, Scene 1) will protect him; but when he hears that 'The wood began to move' his confidence is shaken, and he begins

> To doubt the equivocation of the fiend
> That lies like truth.

At this point we should remember the 'equivocator' that the Porter joked about, long ago, in *Act 2*, Scene 3, and appreciate the way that this whole play insists on the difference between *being* and *seeming*, or between saying one thing and meaning another.

SCENE 6   Continuous battle is now being waged, and the stage should never be
to   empty. Macbeth is at last forced to confront Macduff, and also to
SCENE 9   confront the truth and admit that 'these juggling fiends' cannot be trusted. When the castle has been surrendered, Macbeth defeated, and victory proclaimed, Malcolm announces the beginning of a new reign. Order has now been restored to Scotland, and affairs will once again be conducted 'in measure, time, and place'.

Macbeth: The man

Who can tell us more about a man's character than his wife? Shakespeare allows Lady Macbeth to explain her husband's character as she understands it, and although she cannot see the *whole* truth, she tells us a great deal about Macbeth that *is* true. Two lines of her soliloquy in *Act 1*, Scene 5 are particularly significant:

> Thou wouldst be great,
> Art not without ambition, but without
> The illness should attend it.   (1, 5, 17–19)

By 'illness' Lady Macbeth means 'evil', but her metaphor is appropriate: Macbeth 'catches' evil, as one might catch a disease. The play shows how his symptoms develop, until there is no hope of a cure, and the man must die.

We hear a lot about Macbeth before he comes on to the stage, first from the Sergeant who has fought on his side, and then from Ross, who also speaks of Macbeth's courage in battle. These reports lead us to expect a noble warrior and a loyal subject to Duncan. We have only one slight doubt about Macbeth, and we are not able to explain quite what this is. We know that, somehow, he is associated with the witches; and this, surely, cannot be good.

Macbeth speaks very little when first the witches, and then Ross, hail him as 'thane of Cawdor'. Perhaps he is stunned to silence by his good fortune. But soon we hear him speak—or rather, think aloud, for he does not mean to be overheard:

> Glamis, and Thane of Cawdor:
> The greatest is behind.   (1, 3, 115–16)

Very soon he begins to admit a 'suggestion', some 'horrible imaginings', and then he says to himself the word 'murder' (1, 3, 133; 137; 138). Once this word has been spoken, we must regard Macbeth with suspicion, and the suspicion grows when he confesses his 'black and deep desires' in the scene that follows (1, 4, 51). It is confirmed when his wife, speaking as though he were in the room with her, tells Macbeth that she knows he wants

> that which rather thou dost fear to do,
> Than wishest should be undone.   (1, 5, 23–4)

It is not, however, cowardice that restrains Macbeth. At the end of *Act 1* he is wrestling with his conscience. He is acutely aware of the duty which he owes to Duncan:

> He's here in double trust:
> First, as I am his kinsman and his subject,
> Strong both against the deed; then, as his host,
> Who should against his murderer shut the door,
> Not bear the knife myself.   (1, 7, 12–16)

These are profound reasons for curbing his ambition, but Macbeth continues the soliloquy. Even if he were not—as kinsman, subject, and host—in duty bound to defend Duncan, rather than harm him, there would still be enormous sin in killing the king. Macbeth appreciates Duncan's fine qualities—his humility and his integrity in carrying out to perfection the tasks of kingship; and he knows that to destroy such virtue would be a crime against heaven. He can appreciate Duncan's good qualities and this is a virtue in Macbeth.

Before Lady Macbeth comes on to the scene, Macbeth has won a great victory over himself, and he is almost triumphant when he tells her, 'We will proceed no further in this business' (1, 7, 31).

But Lady Macbeth has no such conscience as her husband has. At this moment she is the stronger of the two, and Macbeth cannot stand up to her accusations that he is a coward, lacking in manliness, and a traitor to his word. He yields to her, and in order to prove himself a man in her eyes, submits to a woman's guidance.

After the murder of Duncan, Macbeth is horrified to think of what he has done. Again Shakespeare contrasts Macbeth and his wife in their attitudes to murder. Lady Macbeth is bold and confident, because she does not understand that the deed is morally wrong; her only concern is to destroy the evidence. Macbeth, however, awakens to a consciousness of guilt that will remain with him until his death.

Macbeth now has to act many parts. When the body of Duncan is discovered, he must appear as the loyal subject, appalled by the murder of his king. In speaking to the two Murderers whom he has hired to kill Banquo, he tries to show that he is a worthy ruler, distressed by injuries which have been inflicted on his subjects. And at the state banquet, probably his first public appearance since he was made king, he plays the part of host and friend to his thanes. He is not wholly successful in any of these roles. When the murder is discovered, he over-acts to such an extent that his wife tries to draw attention from him by fainting. The Murderers are not interested in his efforts to justify the murder of

Banquo: they have been hired to kill a man, and they will do the job they are paid to do. And the banquet is ruined for Macbeth by the appearance of Banquo's Ghost.

Macbeth appears again as himself (that is, not playing any 'part') at the end of *Act 3*, Scene 4, when he and his wife face each other across the remains of their banquet. He now knows that 'blood will have blood' (3, 4, 122), and that the first murder is *only* the first. A new character is emerging—a man who is so desperate that he must act and not stop to consider the reasons for acting:

> Strange things I have in head that will to hand,
> Which must be acted ere they may be scann'd.   (3, 4, 139–40)

The last line here refers to an actor's part in a play, which ought to be 'scann'd'—learned—before it is performed. With this comparison, Macbeth is beginning to recognize an unreality about his life.

The new Macbeth confronts the witches and demands to be answered; the answers give him a feeling of confidence which we, the audience, know to be unfounded. But Macbeth trusts no one. He has no faith in the loyalty of the thanes, and sets spies on each one of them (see 3, 4, 131–2); now it seems that he will not trust even the witches and their 'masters', for he is determined to 'make assurance double sure' (4, 1, 82) by slaughtering Macduff's entire family.

We do not see Macbeth for some time after his appearance in this scene with the witches. We hear a lot about him—and everything that we hear tells us that Macbeth has become a cruel tyrant, and that he has changed Scotland into a country 'Almost afraid to know itself' (4, 3, 167). There are more rumours to be heard when Malcolm's army moves towards Dunsinane, and we learn that opinions about Macbeth vary—but only slightly:

> Some say he's mad; others that lesser hate him
> Do call it valiant fury.   (5, 2, 13–14)

He is indeed madly self-confident, believing that he is invincible:

> Till Birnam Wood remove to Dunsinane,
> I cannot taint with fear. What's the boy Malcolm?
> Was he not born of woman?   (5, 3, 2–4)

Alone, however, Macbeth is neither mad nor furious. He feels old and lonely:

> My way of life
> Is fall'n into the sere, the yellow leaf,
> And that which should accompany old age,
> As honour, love, obedience, troops of friends,
> I must not look to have. (5, 3, 22–6)

Seyton tells him that his wife is dead, but he cannot grieve for her. Life has no meaning for him, and once again he sees himself as an actor,

> That struts and frets his hour upon the stage
> And then is heard no more. (5, 5, 24–5)

He has lost everything, and when he hears of the 'moving grove' (5, 5, 37) he knows that he is defeated.

Macbeth chooses to die in battle, 'with harness on our back' (5, 5, 51), and the decision perhaps revives a spark of our former respect for the mighty warrior. At last he is challenged by Macduff, and he is reluctant to fight:

> Of all men else I have avoided thee,
> But get thee back, my soul is too much charg'd
> With blood of thine already. (5, 8, 4–6)

How should we interpret this? The first of the Apparitions told Macbeth to 'Beware Macduff'—is this why he has avoided him? Or is it guilt that has kept Macbeth from coming face-to-face with the man whose wife and children have been so brutally murdered? Is conscience returning with courage?

Shakespeare's Verse

Easily the best way to understand and appreciate Shakespeare's verse is to read it aloud—and don't worry if you don't understand everything! Try not to be captivated by the dominant rhythm, but decide which are the most important words in each line and use the regular metre to drive them forward to the listeners.

Shakespeare's plays are mainly written in 'blank verse', the form preferred by most dramatists in the sixteenth and early seventeenth centuries. It is a very flexible medium, which is capable—like the human speaking voice—of a wide range of tones. Basically the lines, which are unrhymed, are ten syllables long. The syllables have alternating stresses, just like normal English speech; and they divide into five 'feet'. The technical name for this is 'iambic pentameter'.

> **Macbeth**
> So foúl and faír a dáy I háve not seén.
> **Banquo**
> How fár is't cáll'd to Fórres? Whát are thése,
> So wíther'd ánd so wíld in théir attíre,
> That loók not líke th'inhábitants ó'th'eárth,
> And yét are ón't?—Live yóu, or áre you aúght
> That mán may quéstion? You seém to únderstánd me,
> By eách at ónce her chóppy fínger láying
> Upón her skínny líps; you shóuld be wómen,
> And yét your beárds forbíd me tó intérpret
> That yóu are só.
> **Macbeth**
>   Speak íf you cán: what áre you?

1, 3, 36–45

Here the pentameter accommodates a variety of speech tones— Macbeth is casual in his conversation about the weather; Banquo is surprised at the appearance of these creatures, and fearful that they may be supernatural beings; he is comforted when they seem to understand him; and he can even make a nervous joke about their beards. Macbeth, speaking with some authority, completes a line started by Banquo— and so identifies himself with the other's feelings. Some words in Banquo's speech have had to be elided ('th'inhabitants', 'o'th'), but this is usual in English—especially when the speaker is under pressure from some emotion (and Banquo is *very* surprised!).

In this quotation, the lines are mainly regular in length and normal in iambic stress pattern. Sometimes Shakespeare deviates from the norm, writing lines that are longer or shorter than ten syllables, and varying the stress patterns for unusual emphasis. The verse line sometimes contains the grammatical unit of meaning—'So wither'd and so wild in their attire'—thus allowing for a pause at the end of the line, before a new idea is started; at other times, the sense runs on from one line to the next—'are you aught That man may question'. This makes for the natural fluidity of speech, avoiding monotony but still maintaining the iambic rhythm.

Source, Date, and Text

Raphael Holinshed's *Chronicles of Scotland* (1577) provided most of the material Shakespeare needed for the writing of *Macbeth*—which was probably in the summer of 1606. The evidence for this date comes partly from within the play itself, where the drunken Porter in *Act 2, Scene 3* imagines himself to be functioning at the gate of hell. Among the damned sinners he admits is a certain 'equivocator', who has 'committed treason enough for God's sake' but who has not been able 'to equivocate to heaven'. This is a reference to a certain Father Garnet, a Jesuit priest who was tried and executed in the spring of 1606 for his part in the Gunpowder Plot to blow up the King and the Houses of Parliament on 5th November in the previous year. Father Garnet was known to have prayed for 'the good success of this great action, concerning the Catholic cause, in the beginning of Parliament', and then denied that his prayer had any reference to the Plot, affirming that such equivocation might be confirmed by oath or sacrament without perjury—if necessity required it.

The play did not appear in print until the First Folio collection of Shakespeare's *Works* was published in 1623. The text here shows some signs of revision (perhaps by Shakespeare himself) and adaptation (probably after Shakespeare's death); certainly one scene (3, 5) has been added, and another (4, 1) has been adjusted, both of them accommodating songs from *The Witch*, a much later play of uncertain date by Thomas Middleton.

The present edition is based on the text established by A. R. Braunmuller for the New Cambridge Shakespeare (1997).

People in the Play

Duncan	*King of Scotland*
Malcolm Donaldbain	*his sons*
Macbeth Banquo	*commanders of the Scottish army*
Macduff Lennox Ross Menteith Angus Caithness	*thanes of Scotland* (*thane*: a Scottish nobleman, just below the rank of earl in the English nobility.)
Fleance	Banquo*'s son*
Boy	Macduff*'s son*
Seyton	*an officer attending* Macbeth
Siward	*Earl of Northumberland, commander of the English army*
Young Siward	*his son*
Lady Macbeth	
Lady Macduff	
Three Witches	

A Captain
A Porter
An Old Man
Three Murderers
An English Doctor
A Scottish Doctor
A Gentlewoman attending Lady Macbeth
Hecate *goddess and queen of witches*
The Ghost of Banquo
Apparitions
Lords, Attendants, Soldiers, Servants, Messengers

'Fair is foul, and foul is fair', (1, 1, 12). Aicha Kossoko, Amanda Harris, and Joyce Henderson as the three Witches, Battersea Arts Centre, 2000.

ACT 1

Act 1 Scene 1
A Prologue of evil: the three witches arrange to meet Macbeth when the fighting is over.

SCENE 1

The battlefield: thunder and lightning. Enter three Witches

First Witch
When shall we three meet again?
In thunder, lightning, or in rain?
Second Witch
When the hurly-burly's done,
When the battle's lost, and won.
Third Witch
5 That will be ere the set of sun.
First Witch
Where the place?
Second Witch
Upon the heath.
Third Witch
There to meet with Macbeth.
First Witch
I come, Graymalkin.
Second Witch
10 Paddock calls.
Third Witch
Anon.
All
Fair is foul, and foul is fair,
Hover through the fog and filthy air.   [*Exeunt*

3 *hurly-burly*: turmoil, tumult.
4 *When . . . won*: Winning and losing will become a major theme in the play.

7 *heath*: moorland, wilderness.

9 *Graymalkin*: grey cat; the Witch answers her attendant spirit ('familiar').
10 *Paddock*: toad.

11 *anon*: I'm coming.

12 *Fair . . . fair*: This paradox (= contradiction in terms) will recur throughout the play.
13 *Exeunt*: Directors of the play have found many different ways for the witches to leave the stage—either on foot through a stage door or a trap-door, or by some kind of flying. See *1*, 5, 4–5.

Act 1 Scene 2
King Duncan hears good news of the battle:
Banquo and Macbeth have fought valiantly
against his enemies, and the king rewards
Macbeth with a new title.

0s.d. *Alarum*: A trumpet call to arms;
this is enough to identify the scene's
location.
within: offstage.

2 *as . . . plight*: his condition suggests.

3 *newest*: latest.
sergeant: This was a higher rank than
it is today.

5 *'Gainst my captivity*: so that I was not
captured.
6 *broil*: conflict.

8 *spent*: exhausted.

9 *choke their art*: defeat their own
efforts.
10 *Worthy . . . rebel*: only fit to be a
traitor.
for to that: because.
11 *villainies of nature*: evils within
creation.
12–13 *from . . . supplied*: had
reinforcements of foot-soldiers
('kerns') and fighting-men with battle-
axes ('galloglasses') from Ireland and
the Hebrides ('the Western Isles').
14 *damned*: damnèd.
15 *a rebel's whore*: a treacherous
prostitute.
18 *smok'd*: steamed.
19 *minion*: favourite.
21 *ne'er shook hands*: never parted from
him.
22 *unseam'd . . . chaps*: ripped him open
from navel to jaws.

25–8 *As . . . swells*: just as stormy
weather can come from the east, so
further trouble arose from a source
which should have brought help.
25 *'gins his reflection*: begins shining.

SCENE 2

The king's headquarters: alarum within. Enter King
Duncan, Malcolm, Donaldbain, Lennox, *with*
Attendants, *meeting a bleeding* Captain

Duncan
What bloody man is that? He can report,
As seemeth by his plight, of the revolt
The newest state.
Malcolm
                    This is the sergeant
Who like a good and hardy soldier fought
5 'Gainst my captivity. Hail, brave friend;
Say to the king the knowledge of the broil
As thou didst leave it.
Captain
                    Doubtful it stood,
As two spent swimmers that do cling together
And choke their art. The merciless Macdonald—
10 Worthy to be a rebel, for to that
The multiplying villainies of nature
Do swarm upon him—from the Western Isles
Of kerns and galloglasses is supplied,
And Fortune on his damned quarrel smiling,
15 Show'd like a rebel's whore. But all's too weak,
For brave Macbeth—well he deserves that name—
Disdaining Fortune, with his brandish'd steel,
Which smok'd with bloody execution,
Like Valour's minion carv'd out his passage
20 Till he fac'd the slave,
Which ne'er shook hands, nor bade farewell to him,
Till he unseam'd him from the nave to th'chaps
And fix'd his head upon our battlements.
Duncan
O valiant cousin, worthy gentleman.
Captain
25 As whence the sun 'gins his reflection,
Shipwrecking storms and direful thunders,
So from that spring whence comfort seem'd to come,
Discomfort swells. Mark, King of Scotland, mark,

No sooner justice had, with valour arm'd,

30 *Compell'd . . . heels*: forced these panic-stricken ruffians to run away.

31 *the Norwegian lord*: i.e. Sweno, King of Norway (who invaded Scotland in 1041).
surveying vantage: seizing his advantage.

32 *furbish'd arms*: reinforced armaments.

36 *sooth*: truth.

37 *double cracks*: twice as much ammunition as usual.

39 *Except*: unless.
reeking: steaming with blood.

40 *memorize . . . Golgotha*: make this scene of bloodshed as memorable as the scene of Christ's crucifixion.

44 *smack*: taste.

45 *Thane*: the head of the clan (= Scottish family or tribe).

46 *What . . . eyes*: his eyes look as though he is in a hurry.

49 *flout*: mock; the Norwegian flags had no right to be in Fife.

51 *Norway himself*: the king of Norway.
54 *Bellona's bridegroom*: Macbeth, looking like the husband of the Roman goddess of war.
lapp'd in proof: clad in strong armour.

30 Compell'd these skipping kerns to trust their heels,
But the Norwegian lord, surveying vantage,
With furbish'd arms and new supplies of men
Began a fresh assault.
Duncan
Dismay'd not this our captains, Macbeth and Banquo?
Captain
35 Yes, as sparrows, eagles, or the hare, the lion.
If I say sooth, I must report they were
As cannons over-charg'd with double cracks;
So they doubly redoubled strokes upon the foe.
Except they meant to bathe in reeking wounds
40 Or memorize another Golgotha,
I cannot tell.
But I am faint, my gashes cry for help.
Duncan
So well thy words become thee as thy wounds;
They smack of honour both. Go get him surgeons.
                    [*Exit* Captain, *attended*

Enter Ross *and* Angus

45 Who comes here?
Malcolm
                    The worthy Thane of Ross.
Lennox
What a haste looks through his eyes! So should he look
That seems to speak things strange.
Ross
                              God save the king.
Duncan
Whence cam'st thou, worthy thane?
Ross
                              From Fife, great king,
Where the Norwegian banners flout the sky
50 And fan our people cold.
Norway himself, with terrible numbers,
Assisted by that most disloyal traitor,
The Thane of Cawdor, began a dismal conflict,
Till that Bellona's bridegroom, lapp'd in proof,

55 *self-comparisons*: equal terms.
56 *Point*: sword.
57 *lavish*: unrestrained, impetuous.

59 *craves composition*: seeks to make peace.
61 *disbursed*: disbursèd; paid.
Saint Colm's Inch: Inchcolm, an island in the Firth of Forth.
62 *dollars*: silver coins (German *thaler*).
64 *bosom interest*: trusting confidence.
present death: immediate death sentence.

65 *former title*: i.e. 'Thane of Cawdor'; see '*Macbeth*: the source', p.101.

67 *lost . . . won*: See *1, 1, 4*.

Act 1 Scene 3
The Witches speak strange prophecies to Macbeth and Banquo—and the first prophecy comes true.

2 *Killing swine*: Witches were often accused of harming livestock.

4 *quoth*: said.
5 *Aroint*: get away with you.
rump-fed runnion: fat-bottomed old woman; the abusive expression (Shakespeare's own coinage) has no specific meaning.
6 *Aleppo*: A trading city in northern Syria.
master: captain.
Tiger: A common name for a ship.
7 *sieve . . . sail*: This was thought to be common practice for witches.
9 *do*: work on him; the witch probably intends some kind of fornication.

---

55 Confronted him with self-comparisons,
 Point against point, rebellious arm 'gainst arm,
 Curbing his lavish spirit. And to conclude,
 The victory fell on us—
  Duncan
          Great happiness!—
  Ross
               That now Sweno,
 The Norways' king, craves composition.
60 Nor would we deign him burial of his men
 Till he disbursed at Saint Colm's Inch
 Ten thousand dollars to our general use.
  Duncan
 No more that Thane of Cawdor shall deceive
 Our bosom interest. Go pronounce his present death
65 And with his former title greet Macbeth.
  Ross
 I'll see it done.
  Duncan
 What he hath lost, noble Macbeth hath won.   [*Exeunt*

SCENE 3

The heath: thunder. Enter the three Witches

  First Witch
 Where hast thou been, sister?
  Second Witch
 Killing swine.
  Third Witch
          Sister, where thou?
  First Witch
 A sailor's wife had chestnuts in her lap
 And munch'd, and munch'd, and munch'd. 'Give me',
   quoth I.
5 'Aroint thee, witch', the rump-fed runnion cries.
 Her husband's to Aleppo gone, master o'th'Tiger:
 But in a sieve I'll thither sail,
 And like a rat without a tail,
 I'll do, I'll do, and I'll do.

10 *give . . . wind*: Witches were believed to have power to control the winds.

13 *the other*: i.e. the other winds.
14 *the very . . . blow*: even the ports where these winds blow (so that the ships cannot take refuge).
15 *quarters*: directions.
16 *card*: compass, chart.
17 *drain him*: exhaust him (probably with enforced sexual intercourse).
19 *penthouse lid*: eyelid (overhanging his eye).
20 *forbid*: cursed.
21 *sennights*: weeks.
22 *peak, and pine*: waste away.
23 *bark*: ship.
cannot be lost: The witches could injure human beings, but not kill them.

30 *weïrd*: supernatural, mystic.
31 *Posters*: high-speed travellers.

33 *to thine*: in your direction.

35 *wound up*: complete.

Second Witch
10 I'll give thee a wind.
    First Witch
Thou'rt kind.
    Third Witch
And I another.
    First Witch
I myself have all the other,
And the very ports they blow,
15 All the quarters that they know
I'th'shipman's card.
I'll drain him dry as hay:
Sleep shall neither night nor day
Hang upon his penthouse lid;
20 He shall live a man forbid.
Weary sennights nine times nine,
Shall he dwindle, peak, and pine.
Though his bark cannot be lost,
Yet it shall be tempest-toss'd.
25 Look what I have.
    Second Witch
                    Show me, show me.
    First Witch
Here I have a pilot's thumb,
Wreck'd as homeward he did come.

Drum within

    Third Witch
A drum, a drum;
Macbeth doth come.
    All
30 The weïrd sisters, hand in hand,
Posters of the sea and land,
Thus do go, about, about,
Thrice to thine, and thrice to mine,
And thrice again, to make up nine.
35 Peace, the charm's wound up.

36 *foul and fair*: i.e. the weather has
   been foul but their fighting has been
   successful.
37–67 See '*Macbeth*: the source', p.101.
37 *How . . . Forres*: how far do you reckon
   we are from Forres.

42 *choppy*: chapped.

46 *Glamis*: This word is usually
   pronounced as a single syllable,
   'Glahms'.
47 *Thane of Cawdor*: The audience knows
   already that Macbeth has been given
   this title (see *1, 2, 65*).

49 *start*: flinch, recoil.

51 *fantastical*: imaginary.
52–5 *My . . . withal*: you greet my noble
   friend with the title he already has
   and with such prophecy of further
   ennoblement and even royal status
   that he seems amazed with it all.

56 *seeds of time*: sources of the future.

Enter Macbeth *and* Banquo

Macbeth
So foul and fair a day I have not seen.
  Banquo
How far is't called to Forres? What are these,
So wither'd and so wild in their attire,
That look not like th'inhabitants o'th'earth,
40 And yet are on't?—Live you, or are you aught
That man may question? You seem to understand me,
By each at once her choppy finger laying
Upon her skinny lips; you should be women,
And yet your beards forbid me to interpret
45 That you are so.
  Macbeth   Speak if you can: what are you?
  First Witch
All hail Macbeth, hail to thee, Thane of Glamis.
  Second Witch
All hail Macbeth, hail to thee, Thane of Cawdor.
  Third Witch
All hail Macbeth, that shalt be king hereafter.
  Banquo
Good sir, why do you start and seem to fear
50 Things that do sound so fair?—I'th'name of truth
Are ye fantastical, or that indeed
Which outwardly ye show? My noble partner
You greet with present grace and great prediction
Of noble having and of royal hope
55 That he seems rapt withal. To me you speak not.
If you can look into the seeds of time
And say which grain will grow and which will not,
Speak then to me, who neither beg nor fear
Your favours nor your hate.
  First Witch
60 Hail.
  Second Witch
Hail.

Third Witch
Hail.
First Witch
Lesser than Macbeth, and greater.
Second Witch
Not so happy, yet much happier.
Third Witch
65 Thou shalt get kings, though thou be none.
So all hail Macbeth and Banquo.
First Witch
Banquo and Macbeth, all hail.
Macbeth
Stay, you imperfect speakers. Tell me more.
By Finel's death, I know I am Thane of Glamis,
70 But how of Cawdor? The Thane of Cawdor lives
A prosperous gentleman, and to be king
Stands not within the prospect of belief,
No more than to be Cawdor. Say from whence
You owe this strange intelligence, or why
75 Upon this blasted heath you stop our way
With such prophetic greeting? Speak, I charge you.

Witches *vanish*

Banquo
The earth hath bubbles, as the water has,
And these are of them. Whither are they vanish'd?
Macbeth
Into the air, and what seem'd corporal,
80 Melted, as breath into the wind. Would they had stay'd.
Banquo
Were such things here as we do speak about?
Or have we eaten on the insane root,
That takes the reason prisoner?
Macbeth
Your children shall be kings.
Banquo
                                        You shall be king.
Macbeth
85 And Thane of Cawdor too: went it not so?

64 *happy*: fortunate.

65 *get*: beget, father.

68 *imperfect*: obscure, ambiguous.
69 *Finel*: Macbeth's father.
70–1 *The Thane . . . gentleman*: Shakespeare seems to have forgotten that Macbeth has just been fighting Cawdor (*1, 2, 54–7*).
72 *Stands . . . belief*: is unbelievable.
74 *intelligence*: information.
75 *blasted*: blighted, barren.
76 *charge*: command.

79 *corporal*: substantial, having a body.
80 *Would*: I wish.

82 *insane root*: hemlock (which was thought to cause madness).

Banquo
To th'selfsame tune and words—who's here?

Enter Ross *and* Angus

Ross
The king hath happily receiv'd, Macbeth,
The news of thy success, and when he reads
Thy personal venture in the rebels' sight,
90 His wonders and his praises do contend
Which should be thine or his. Silenc'd with that,
In viewing o'er the rest o'th'selfsame day,
He finds thee in the stout Norwegian ranks,
Nothing afeard of what thyself didst make,
95 Strange images of death. As thick as tale
Came post with post, and every one did bear
Thy praises in his kingdom's great defence,
And pour'd them down before him.
Angus
                                                    We are sent
To give thee from our royal master thanks;
100 Only to herald thee into his sight,
Not pay thee.
        Ross
And for an earnest of a greater honour,
He bade me, from him, call thee Thane of Cawdor:
In which addition, hail most worthy thane,
105 For it is thine.
        Banquo
                            What, can the devil speak true?
        Macbeth
The Thane of Cawdor lives. Why do you dress me
In borrow'd robes?
        Angus
                                Who was the thane, lives yet,
But under heavy judgement bears that life
Which he deserves to lose.
110 Whether he was combin'd with those of Norway,
Or did line the rebel with hidden help
And vantage, or that with both he labour'd
In his country's wrack, I know not,

88 *reads*: recognizes.
89 *venture*: achievement.
90–1 *His wonders . . . his*: he doesn't know whether to be silent in wonder or speak out in your praises.
92 *selfsame*: that very same.
93 *stout*: valiant.
94 *Nothing afeard*: not at all frightened.
95–6 *As thick . . . post*: one messenger ('post') followed another, and every one brought a new tale.

98–101 *We . . . thee*: Ross and Angus have been sent to bring Macbeth into the king's presence and to express Duncan's thanks—which will not be Macbeth's only reward.

102 *earnest*: foretaste.

104 *addition*: title.

106–7 *dress . . . robes*: Clothes and images of clothing are very important throughout the play—and perhaps Ross invests Macbeth with some garment symbolic of his new title.
107 *Who*: he who.

111 *line*: reinforce (like the lining of a garment).
112 *vantage*: advantage (perhaps the traitor provided a base in Scotland for the foreign enemy's attack).
113 *wrack*: ruin, overthrow.

114 *capital*: deserving capital punishment.

116 *The greatest is behind*: the greatest prophecy is the last one, and has yet to come true.
pains: trouble.
118 *those . . . me*: those who promised me the title 'Thane of Cawdor'.

119 *home*: completely.
120 *enkindle . . . crown*: fire you to strive for the crown.

122–5 *oftentimes . . . consequence*: often, to bring about our damnation, the agents of evil tell us simple truths to make us trust them, then they can deceive us in important matters.

126 *Cousins*: friends.

127–8 *prologues . . . theme*: Macbeth anticipates a mighty drama on the theme of kingship.
129–36 *This . . . nature*: Macbeth's uncertainty expresses itself in the 'seesaw' rhythms of these disturbing lines.
129 *soliciting*: persuasion.

135 *seated*: firmly fixed.
138–40 *My thought . . . surmise*: the very thought—although it's only a fantasy—shakes my entire being, and I can do nothing without thinking of it; Macbeth's state of mind is expressed as much in the irregular grammar as in the meanings of his words.
140–1 *nothing . . . is not*: nothing matters now except what is yet to come.
141 *rapt*: entranced; Banquo has already used this word to describe Macbeth (line 55).

143 *Without my stir*: Without any effort from me.

But treasons capital, confess'd and prov'd,
115 Have overthrown him.
    Macbeth
[*Aside*]   Glamis, and Thane of Cawdor:
The greatest is behind.—Thanks for your pains.—
[*To* Banquo] Do you not hope your children shall be kings,
When those that gave the Thane of Cawdor to me
Promis'd no less to them?
    Banquo
                    That trusted home,
120 Might yet enkindle you unto the crown,
Besides the Thane of Cawdor. But 'tis strange,
And oftentimes, to win us to our harm,
The instruments of darkness tell us truths;
Win us with honest trifles, to betray's
125 In deepest consequence.—
Cousins, a word, I pray you.
    Macbeth
[*Aside*]   Two truths are told,
As happy prologues to the swelling act
Of the imperial theme.—I thank you, gentlemen.—
This supernatural soliciting
130 Cannot be ill, cannot be good. If ill,
Why hath it given me earnest of success,
Commencing in a truth? I am Thane of Cawdor.
If good, why do I yield to that suggestion,
Whose horrid image doth unfix my hair
135 And make my seated heart knock at my ribs
Against the use of nature? Present fears
Are less than horrible imaginings.
My thought, whose murder yet is but fantastical,
Shakes so my single state of man that function
140 Is smother'd in surmise, and nothing is,
But what is not.
    Banquo
             Look how our partner's rapt.
    Macbeth
If chance will have me king, why chance may crown me
Without my stir.

144–5 *Like . . . use*: like new clothes that
   don't fit our bodies until we are used
   to them.
   cleave: cling.

146 *Time . . . day*: 'The longest day has an
   end' (proverbial).

147 *stay . . . leisure*: wait until you're free.

148 *favour*: indulgence.
   wrought: agitated, perplexed.
149 *pains*: kindnesses, services.
150–1 *register'd . . . them*: recorded in my
   memory like a book that I read every
   day.
151 *leaf*: page of a book.
152 *chanc'd*: happened.
   at more time: when we have more
   time, later.
153 *The . . . weigh'd it*: having thoroughly
   considered it in the meantime
   ('interim').
154 *free hearts*: what we really feel.

Banquo
                        New honours come upon him
Like our strange garments, cleave not to their mould,
145 But with the aid of use.
   Macbeth
                              Come what come may,
Time and the hour runs through the roughest day.
   Banquo
Worthy Macbeth, we stay upon your leisure.
   Macbeth
Give me your favour. My dull brain was wrought
With things forgotten. Kind gentlemen, your pains
150 Are register'd where every day I turn
The leaf to read them. Let us toward the king.
[*To* Banquo] Think upon what hath chanc'd and at
   more time,
The interim having weigh'd it, let us speak
Our free hearts each to other.
   Banquo
                              Very gladly.
   Macbeth
155 Till then, enough.—Come, friends.   [*Exeunt*

Act 1 Scene 4
King Duncan receives Macbeth and Banquo with gratitude for their achievements, then announces that his son Malcolm will succeed him on the throne of Scotland.

0s.d. *Flourish*: A fanfare heralding the approach of royalty.

1 *done*: carried out.
or not: or are not.
2 *in commission*: in charge of the execution.
liege: lord.

6 *set forth*: showed, professed.

8 *Became*: graced, befitted.
9 *studied*: practised.
10 *ow'd*: owned.
11 As *'twere*: as though it were.

SCENE 4

The king's headquarters. Flourish. Enter King Duncan, Lennox, Malcolm, Donaldbain, *and* Attendants

Duncan
Is execution done on Cawdor, or not
Those in commission yet return'd?
Malcolm
                                    My liege,
They are not yet come back. But I have spoke
With one that saw him die, who did report
5 That very frankly he confess'd his treasons,
Implor'd your highness' pardon, and set forth
A deep repentance. Nothing in his life
Became him like the leaving it. He died
As one that had been studied in his death,
10 To throw away the dearest thing he ow'd
As 'twere a careless trifle.

11–12 *There's . . . face*: there's no way of
telling what's in a man's mind just by
looking on his face; the truth of this
judgement will be demonstrated many
times during the play.
12 *construction*: composition.

Duncan

There's no art
To find the mind's construction in the face.
He was a gentleman on whom I built
An absolute trust.

Enter Macbeth, Banquo, Ross, *and* Angus

O worthiest cousin,
15 The sin of my ingratitude even now
Was heavy on me. Thou art so far before,
That swiftest wing of recompense is slow
To overtake thee. Would thou hadst less deserv'd,
That the proportion both of thanks and payment
20 Might have been mine. Only I have left to say,
More is thy due than more than all can pay.
    Macbeth
The service and the loyalty I owe,
In doing it, pays itself. Your highness' part
Is to receive our duties, and our duties
25 Are to your throne and state, children and servants,
Which do but what they should by doing everything
Safe toward your love and honour.
    Duncan
                        Welcome hither.
I have begun to plant thee and will labour
To make thee full of growing. Noble Banquo,
30 That hast no less deserv'd, nor must be known
No less to have done so, let me enfold thee
And hold thee to my heart.
    Banquo
                        There if I grow,
The harvest is your own.
    Duncan
                        My plenteous joys,
Wanton in fullness, seek to hide themselves
35 In drops of sorrow. Sons, kinsmen, thanes,
And you whose places are the nearest, know:
We will establish our estate upon
Our eldest, Malcolm, whom we name hereafter
The Prince of Cumberland, which honour must

16 *before*: in doing deeds of merit.

18–20 *Would . . . mine*: I wish you
deserved less, so that my rewards
might have been in proportion.

23 *pays itself*: is its own reward.

26–7 *Which . . . honour*: it is no more
than our duty to do everything we can
to protect your love and honour.

30–1 *nor . . . less*: and must also be
recognized to have deserved as much.

34 *Wanton*: lavish, profuse.

36 *nearest*: most closely related.
39 *Prince of Cumberland*: The title of the
Scottish heir apparent (the equivalent
of the English 'Prince of Wales'); see
'*Macbeth*: the source', p.101.

42 *Inverness*: i.e. to Macbeth's castle.

40 Not unaccompanied invest him only,
But signs of nobleness like stars shall shine
On all deservers. [*To* Macbeth] From hence to
    Inverness
And bind us further to you.
        Macbeth
The rest is labour which is not us'd for you;
45 I'll be myself the harbinger and make joyful
The hearing of my wife with your approach.
So humbly take my leave.
        Duncan
                              My worthy Cawdor.
        Macbeth
[*Aside*] The Prince of Cumberland: that is a step
On which I must fall down, or else o'erleap,
50 For in my way it lies. Stars, hide your fires,
Let not light see my black and deep desires,
The eye wink at the hand. Yet let that be,
Which the eye fears when it is done to see.   [*Exit*
        Duncan
True, worthy Banquo, he is full so valiant,
55 And in his commendations I am fed;
It is a banquet to me. Let's after him,
Whose care is gone before to bid us welcome:
It is a peerless kinsman.

        Flourish   [*Exeunt*

Notes:

44 *The . . . you*: everything is labour unless it is done for you.
45 *harbinger*: An officer of the royal household sent ahead to procure accommodation for the king.

52 *wink at the hand*: not see what the hand is doing.

54 *True . . . valiant*: Banquo seems to have been praising Macbeth to Duncan—whilst the audience was listening to Macbeth's thoughts, spoken '*aside*'.

Act 1 Scene 5
Lady Macbeth reads her husband's letter before welcoming him home and preparing to receive the king.

2 *perfectest*: most reliable.

5 *rapt*: entranced: compare *1*, 3, 141.
6 *missives*: messengers.
   all-hailed me: greeted me with 'All hail'.

Scene 5

Inverness: Macbeth's castle. Enter Lady Macbeth *alone, with a letter*

        Lady Macbeth
[*Reads*] 'They met me in the day of success, and I have learned by the perfectest report they have more in them than mortal knowledge. When I burned in desire to question them further, they made themselves air, into
5 which they vanished. Whiles I stood rapt in the wonder of it, came missives from the king who all-hailed me

7   *weïrd*: mystic.

10 *deliver*: report to.
11 *dues of rejoicing*: your share of the rejoicing.

16 *milk . . . kindness*: natural compassion characteristic of human beings.
17 *catch*: snatch at.
19 *illness*: wickedness, cruelty.
    attend: accompany.
    highly: dearly.
20 *holily*: righteously.

24 *Hie thee*: hurry.

27 *the golden round*: the crown.
28 *metaphysical*: supernatural.

29 *tidings*: news.

32 *have . . . preparation*: have given warning so that we could make preparations.

34 *had . . . him*: travelled faster than he did.
35 *for breath*: for lack of breath.

Thane of Cawdor, by which title before these weïrd sisters saluted me and referred me to the coming on of time, with "Hail, king that shalt be." This have I thought
10 good to deliver thee, my dearest partner of greatness, that thou mightst not lose the dues of rejoicing by being ignorant of what greatness is promised thee. Lay it to thy heart and farewell.'
Glamis thou art, and Cawdor, and shalt be
15 What thou art promis'd; yet do I fear thy nature,
It is too full o'th'milk of human kindness
To catch the nearest way. Thou wouldst be great,
Art not without ambition, but without
The illness should attend it. What thou wouldst highly,
20 That wouldst thou holily; wouldst not play false,
And yet wouldst wrongly win. Thou'dst have, great Glamis,
That which cries, 'Thus thou must do' if thou have it;
And that which rather thou dost fear to do,
Than wishest should be undone. Hie thee hither,
25 That I may pour my spirits in thine ear
And chastise with the valour of my tongue
All that impedes thee from the golden round,
Which fate and metaphysical aid doth seem
To have thee crown'd withal.

Enter Attendant

                                        What is your tidings?
    Attendant
30 The king comes here tonight.
    Lady Macbeth
                                Thou'rt mad to say it.
Is not thy master with him? Who, were't so,
Would have inform'd for preparation.
    Attendant
So please you, it is true: our thane is coming.
One of my fellows had the speed of him;
35 Who almost dead for breath, had scarcely more
Than would make up his message.

36 *tending*: care, attention.

37 *The raven . . . hoarse*: Lady Macbeth
compares the breathless messenger to
a bird of ill omen, a carrion-eater
always found on battlefields.

40 *unsex me*: take away everything that
makes me a woman.
43 *remorse*: pity, compassion.
44 *compunctious . . . nature*: natural
feelings of conscience.
45 *fell*: fierce.
46 *Th'effect and it*: the intention and its
consequence.
47 *gall*: bile (a bitter fluid secreted in the
liver).
murd'ring ministers: agents of evil.
48 *sightless substances*: Although the
spirits are real ('substances'), they are
invisible.
49 *wait . . . mischief*: lie in wait for
something to go wrong in nature.
thick: dense, darkest.
50 *pall thee*: shroud yourself.
dunnest: murkiest.
54 *by . . . hereafter*: by the salutation
'That shalt be king hereafter'
(1, 3, 48).
57 *The future in the instant*: the future
greatness in the present moment.
62 *beguile*: deceive.
63 *Look like the time*: put on the
appropriate appearance (i.e. of a host
welcoming his guest).

Lady Macbeth

       Give him tending,
He brings great news. [*Exit* Attendant
    The raven himself is hoarse
That croaks the fatal entrance of Duncan
Under my battlements. Come, you spirits
40 That tend on mortal thoughts, unsex me here
And fill me from the crown to the toe topfull
Of direst cruelty; make thick my blood,
Stop up th'access and passage to remorse
That no compunctious visitings of nature
45 Shake my fell purpose nor keep peace between
Th'effect and it. Come to my woman's breasts
And take my milk for gall, you murd'ring ministers,
Wherever in your sightless substances
You wait on nature's mischief. Come, thick night,
50 And pall thee in the dunnest smoke of hell,
That my keen knife see not the wound it makes,
Nor heaven peep through the blanket of the dark,
To cry, 'Hold, hold.'

  Enter Macbeth

     Great Glamis, worthy Cawdor,
Greater than both by the all-hail hereafter,
55 Thy letters have transported me beyond
This ignorant present, and I feel now
The future in the instant.
  Macbeth
       My dearest love,
Duncan comes here tonight.
  Lady Macbeth
        And when goes hence?
  Macbeth
Tomorrow, as he purposes.
  Lady Macbeth
      O never
60 Shall sun that morrow see.
Your face, my thane, is as a book where men
May read strange matters. To beguile the time,
Look like the time, bear welcome in your eye,

'To alter favour ever is to fear. Leave all the rest to me.' (*1*, 5, 71–2) Ian McKellen as Macbeth and Judi Dench as Lady Macbeth, Royal Shakespeare Company, 1976.

65 Your hand, your tongue; look like th'innocent flower,
But be the serpent under't. He that's coming
Must be provided for, and you shall put
This night's great business into my dispatch,
Which shall to all our nights and days to come
Give solely sovereign sway and masterdom.

Macbeth

70 We will speak further—

Lady Macbeth

      Only look up clear;
To alter favour ever is to fear.
Leave all the rest to me.   *[Exeunt*

66 *provided for*: prepared for.
67 *dispatch*: control, management.
69 *solely sovereign sway*: absolute regal command.
70 *clear*: honestly, cheerfully.
71 *To . . . fear*: fear always shows itself in a change of facial expression.

Act 1 Scene 6
King Duncan and his followers approach the castle and are welcomed by Lady Macbeth.

0s.d. *Hautboys*: reed instruments, ancestors of the modern oboe.
torches: An indication that the scene takes place at night.
1 *seat*: setting, situation.
2 *Nimbly*: freshly.
4 *martlet*: house-martin, a summer migrant bird that often nests in churches.
approve: witness, give evidence.

5 *mansionry*: nest-building.
6 *jutty*: projecting part of building.
frieze: decorative band underneath cornice.
7 *coign of vantage*: convenient corner.
8 *pendent*: hanging.
procreant cradle: nest.

SCENE 6

Inverness: approaching Macbeth's *castle. Hautboys, and torches. Enter* King Duncan, Malcolm, Donaldbain, Banquo, Lennox, Macduff, Ross, Angus, *and* Attendants

Duncan

This castle hath a pleasant seat; the air
Nimbly and sweetly recommends itself
Unto our gentle senses.

Banquo

      This guest of summer,
The temple-haunting martlet, does approve
5 By his lov'd mansionry that the heaven's breath
Smells wooingly here. No jutty, frieze,
Buttress, nor coign of vantage but this bird
Hath made his pendent bed and procreant cradle;
Where they most breed and haunt, I have observ'd
10 The air is delicate.

Enter Lady Macbeth

Duncan
See, see, our honour'd hostess.—The love
That follows us sometime is our trouble,
Which still we thank as love. Herein I teach you
How you shall bid God yield us for your pains
15 And thank us for your trouble.
Lady Macbeth
                                    All our service,
In every point twice done and then done double,
Were poor and single business to contend
Against those honours deep and broad wherewith
Your majesty loads our house. For those of old,
20 And the late dignities heap'd up to them,
We rest your hermits.
Duncan
                                Where's the Thane of Cawdor?
We cours'd him at the heels and had a purpose
To be his purveyor, but he rides well,
And his great love, sharp as his spur, hath holp him
25 To his home before us. Fair and noble hostess,
We are your guest tonight.
Lady Macbeth
                                Your servants ever
Have theirs, themselves, and what is theirs in count
To make their audit at your highness' pleasure,
Still to return your own.
Duncan
                                Give me your hand;
30 Conduct me to mine host: we love him highly
And shall continue our graces towards him.
By your leave, hostess.   [*Exeunt*

11–12 *The love . . . love*: sometimes it's a nuisance to have people offering me kindness, but I am always ('still') grateful for it.

13–14 *Herein . . . trouble*: this is my way of teaching you to ask God to reward *me* for the trouble *you* are having to take, and also to thank *me* for providing the occasion for that trouble.

13 *yield*: reward.

16 *In . . . double*: if every part were done twice, and then twice again; Lady Macbeth continues the language of duplication and multiplication begun by the Captain (*1*, 2, 37–8), repeated by the weird sisters (*1*, 3, 33–4), and soon to be reiterated by Macbeth (*1*, 7, 12).

17 *single*: simple.
   contend: compete.

19 *those of old*: those honours bestowed in the past.

20 *late*: recent.

21 *hermits*: persons bound by vow or fee to pray for someone.

22 *cours'd*: chased.

23 *purveyor*: official responsible for provisions and accommodation in the royal household.

24 *holp*: helped.

26–9 *Your . . . own*: your majesty's servants hold everything in trust ('in count') for your majesty; they will give an account ('make their audit') whenever you ask, and will always ('still') return everything back to you.

32 *By your leave*: with your permission (a courteous indication that Duncan is ready to enter the castle).

Act 1 Scene 7
Macbeth leaves the state dinner, suddenly worried by what he is planning to do. But Lady Macbeth stirs up his spirits again.

Os.d. The scene takes place in the passageway between dining hall and kitchen.
Sewer: butler.
divers: various.
service: course of a meal.
over: across, from side to side.
1–2 *If . . . quickly*: if the business of the murder were ended ('done') as soon as the deed is performed ('done'), then it would be a good thing to have it carried out ('done') quickly.
2–4 *if . . . success*: if the assassination could prevent ('trammel up') any further consequences and achieve its success with Duncan's death ('surcease').
4 *that but this blow*: this single blow.
5 *be-all . . . end-all*: all that is needed to end everything.
5–6 *here . . . time*: in this life; Macbeth imagines himself standing in the shallow water ('shoal') of a river-bank.
7 *We'd . . . come*: I would risk the chance of any life after death; Macbeth uses the 'royal plural' when speaking in soliloquy.
jump: hazard, risk; leap over.
8–9 *We . . . instructions*: we are always ('still') punished here because we only ('but') teach others our own crimes—which they commit against us ('the inventor').
10 *even-handed*: impartial.
11 *Commends*: recommends, prescribes.
ingredience: mixture of ingredients.
chalice: ceremonial cup.
12 *in double trust*: a) as a monarch and kinsman; b) as a guest.
16 *Besides*: in addition to that.
17 *borne . . . meek*: exercised his royal powers so modestly.
18 *clear*: faultless, honourable.
18–25 *his virtues . . . wind*: The suggestiveness of these lines is more powerful than their logical sense.
19 *trumpet-tongu'd*: sounding like trumpets.
20 *taking-off*: murder.
21–2 *pity . . . blast*: Macbeth visualizes Pity with all the weakness of a human baby yet able to soar over the blasts of the 'trumpet-tongu'd angels'.

SCENE 7

Inside Macbeth'*s castle. Hautboys. Torches. Enter a* Sewer, *and divers* Servants *with dishes and service over the stage. Then enter* Macbeth

Macbeth
If it were done when 'tis done, then 'twere well
It were done quickly. If th'assassination
Could trammel up the consequence and catch
With his surcease, success, that but this blow
5 Might be the be-all and the end-all—here,
But here, upon this bank and shoal of time,
We'd jump the life to come. But in these cases,
We still have judgement here that we but teach
Bloody instructions, which being taught, return
10 To plague th'inventor. This even-handed justice
Commends th'ingredience of our poison'd chalice
To our own lips. He's here in double trust:
First, as I am his kinsman and his subject,
Strong both against the deed; then, as his host,
15 Who should against his murderer shut the door,
Not bear the knife myself. Besides, this Duncan
Hath borne his faculties so meek, hath been
So clear in his great office, that his virtues
Will plead like angels, trumpet-tongu'd against
20 The deep damnation of his taking-off.
And pity, like a naked newborn babe
Striding the blast, or heaven's cherubin hors'd
Upon the sightless couriers of the air,
Shall blow the horrid deed in every eye,
25 That tears shall drown the wind. I have no spur
To prick the sides of my intent, but only
Vaulting ambition which o'erleaps itself
And falls on th'other—

22–3 *cherubin . . . air*: angels riding on
the invisible winds.
26 *intent*: intention (to murder Duncan).
27–8 *Vaulting . . . other*: Macbeth's
excessive ambition is like a horse that
tries to jump too high and falls on the
other side of the fence.

29 *supp'd*: finished dining.
32–4 *I have . . . gloss*: Macbeth wants to
enjoy the praises he has earned
('bought') as though they were new
clothes (compare *1, 3, 106–7*).
33 *sorts*: social ranks.
35–6 *Was . . . yourself*: Here 'hope' is
both a person, and the garment he
wears.
37 *green and pale*: sickly (as if the 'hope'
had a hangover).
39 *Such*: i.e. as a cowardly drunk with a
hangover, scared at what he had
planned to do when he was drunk.
afeard: afraid.
45 *adage*: Lady Macbeth refers to the
proverb ('The cat would eat fish, but
will not wet her feet').
Prithee: I pray you.
46 *become*: be fitting for.
47 *is none*: is not a man (i.e. he is
subhuman or monstrous).
48 *break*: reveal, mention.
49 *durst*: dared.
51–4 *Nor . . . you*: neither time nor place
was suitable then, yet you would make
them suitable; now they are both
right—and the very fact that they are
right ('that their fitness') makes you
lose your nerve ('unmake you').
52 *adhere*: agree.

Enter Lady Macbeth

How now? What news?

Lady Macbeth
He has almost supp'd. Why have you left the chamber?

Macbeth
30 Hath he ask'd for me?

Lady Macbeth
Know you not, he has?

Macbeth
We will proceed no further in this business.
He hath honour'd me of late, and I have bought
Golden opinions from all sorts of people,
Which would be worn now in their newest gloss,
35 Not cast aside so soon.

Lady Macbeth
Was the hope drunk
Wherein you dress'd yourself? Hath it slept since?
And wakes it now to look so green and pale
At what it did so freely? From this time,
Such I account thy love. Art thou afeard
40 To be the same in thine own act and valour,
As thou art in desire? Wouldst thou have that
Which thou esteem'st the ornament of life,
And live a coward in thine own esteem,
Letting 'I dare not' wait upon 'I would',
45 Like the poor cat i'th'adage?

Macbeth
Prithee, peace.
I dare do all that may become a man;
Who dares do more is none.

Lady Macbeth
What beast was't then
That made you break this enterprise to me?
When you durst do it, then you were a man.
50 And to be more than what you were, you would
Be so much more the man. Nor time, nor place
Did then adhere, and yet you would make both.
They have made themselves and that their fitness now
Does unmake you. I have given suck and know

60 *screw . . . sticking-place*: tighten your courage to the limit; the metaphor is from tightening the strings of a lute (or modern guitar) to tune the instrument.

62-3 *Whereto . . . him*: and his long journey today will all the more quickly encourage him to sleep soundly.

63-7 *his . . . only*: I will overpower ('convince') his two attendants with wine and liquor so that their memory, which should guard the brain, shall be an intoxicated haze ('fume'), and the brain itself—the receptacle of reason—shall be of no more use than an alchemist's distilling-flask ('limbeck').

63 *chamberlains*: attendants in the royal bedchamber.
65 *warder*: guard, watchman.
67 *in swinish sleep*: sleeping like pigs.
68 *drenched*: drenchèd; soaked, sozzled.
70 *put*: blame.
71 *spongy*: sponge-like.
72 *quell*: kill, bloodshed.
73 *mettle*: spirit, courage.
74 *receiv'd*: believed.
76 *very*: own.

55 How tender 'tis to love the babe th
I would, while it was smiling in my
Have pluck'd my nipple from his b
And dash'd the brains out, had I so
As you have done to this.

Macbeth

If we should fail?

Lady Macbeth

We fail?

60 But screw your courage to the sticking-place,
And we'll not fail. When Duncan is asleep,
Whereto the rather shall his day's hard journey
Soundly invite him, his two chamberlains
Will I with wine and wassail so convince
65 That memory, the warder of the brain,
Shall be a fume, and the receipt of reason
A limbeck only. When in swinish sleep
Their drenched natures lies as in a death,
What cannot you and I perform upon
70 Th'unguarded Duncan? What not put upon
His spongy officers, who shall bear the guilt
Of our great quell?

Macbeth

Bring forth men-children only,
For thy undaunted mettle should compose
Nothing but males. Will it not be receiv'd,
75 When we have mark'd with blood those sleepy two
Of his own chamber, and us'd their very daggers,
That they have done't?

Lady Macbeth

Who dares receive it other,
As we shall make our griefs and clamour roar
Upon his death?

Macbeth

I am settled and bend up
80 Each corporal agent to this terrible feat.
Away, and mock the time with fairest show,
False face must hide what the false heart doth know.

[*Exeunt*

who . . . death: who will dare
believe anything else, since we shall
cry out about his death with so much
grief and noise.
79 *settled*: decided.
 bend: brace.
80 *corporal agent*: physical faculty.
81 *mock*: deceive.

ACT 2

Act 2 Scene 1
Banquo and his son Fleance are going to bed when they encounter Macbeth, who is preparing himself for his grim task.

SCENE 1

Macbeth's castle: enter Banquo, *and* Fleance, *with a* Torch-bearer *before him*

Banquo
How goes the night, boy?
    Fleance
The moon is down; I have not heard the clock.
    Banquo
And she goes down at twelve.
    Fleance
                   I take't, 'tis later, sir.
    Banquo
Hold, take my sword.—There's husbandry in heaven,
5 Their candles are all out.—Take thee that too.
A heavy summons lies like lead upon me,
And yet I would not sleep; merciful powers,
Restrain in me the cursed thoughts that nature
Gives way to in repose.

Enter Macbeth, *and a* Servant *with a torch*

                Give me my sword—
10 Who's there?
    Macbeth
A friend.
    Banquo
What, sir, not yet at rest? The king's abed.
He hath been in unusual pleasure
And sent forth great largess to your offices.
15 This diamond he greets your wife withal,

Gives Macbeth *a diamond*

3 *she*: the moon.

4 *husbandry*: economy, good housekeeping.
5 *candles*: the stars.
  that: Banquo, preparing for bed, perhaps gives his cloak to Fleance.
6–7 *A heavy . . . sleep*: I feel as heavy as lead, and my bed is calling to me, but yet I don't want to sleep.
8–9 *Restrain . . . repose*: control the nightmares ('those cursed thoughts') that come when the body is at rest; Banquo is afraid of the thoughts provoked by the witches' prophecies.
8 *cursed*: cursèd.
9 *Give . . . sword*: Banquo is tense and alert even inside the castle.

14 *largess*: presents.
  offices: staff.
15 *withal*: with (a form often used to end a clause or sentence).

16 *shut up*: went to bed, closed up the
   curtains of his bed.

17–19 *Being . . . wrought*: because we
   were not prepared, we had to manage
   with very little ('defect' = deficiency)
   and could not be as generous ('free')
   as we wished.
25 *If . . . 'tis*: if you will follow my advice,
   when the time comes.
26–7 *So . . . augment it*: provided that I
   don't lose honour by trying to increase
   it.
28 *bosom franchis'd*: heart free from
   obligation.
   clear: loyal (to the king).

29 *the while*: meanwhile.

36–7 *sensible . . . sight*: able to be felt
   as well as seen.

39 *heat-oppressed*: heat-oppressèd; over-
   heated, disturbed.

By the name of most kind hostess, and shut up
In measureless content.
   Macbeth
                Being unprepar'd,
Our will became the servant to defect,
Which else should free have wrought.
   Banquo
                      All's well.
20 I dream'd last night of the three weïrd sisters;
To you they have show'd some truth.
   Macbeth
                  I think not of them;
Yet when we can entreat an hour to serve,
We would spend it in some words upon that business,
If you would grant the time.
   Banquo
               At your kind'st leisure.
   Macbeth
25 If you shall cleave to my consent, when 'tis,
It shall make honour for you.
   Banquo
                So I lose none
In seeking to augment it, but still keep
My bosom franchis'd and allegiance clear,
I shall be counsell'd.
   Macbeth
              Good repose the while.
   Banquo
30 Thanks, sir; the like to you.
       [*Exeunt* Banquo, Fleance, *and* Torch-bearer
   Macbeth
[*To* Servant] Go bid thy mistress, when my drink is
   ready,
She strike upon the bell. Get thee to bed. [*Exit* Servant
Is this a dagger which I see before me,
The handle toward my hand? Come, let me clutch thee:
35 I have thee not, and yet I see thee still.
Art thou not, fatal vision, sensible
To feeling as to sight? Or art thou but
A dagger of the mind, a false creation,
Proceeding from the heat-oppressed brain?

40 *yet*: still
     palpable: tangible.

42 *marshall'st me*: are guiding me,
     beckon me.

44–5 *Mine . . . rest*: either my eyes are
     deceived, or else they are better than
     all my other senses.
46 *dudgeon*: hilt, handle.
     gouts: splashes (from the French
     goutte = drop).
48–9 *informs . . . eyes*: takes shape in
     this way before my eyes.

51 *celebrates*: performs the rites
     ('offerings').
52 *Hecate*: goddess of the moon and of
     witchcraft; the name has only two
     syllables here.
53 *Alarum'd*: aroused, called to action
     (see *1, 2, 0s.d.*).
54 *Whose . . . watch*: i.e. the wolf's howl
     tells the time to Murder.
55 *Tarquin's . . . strides*: Murder,
     personified in line 52, is now
     compared to the Roman tyrant,
     Tarquin, who came in the night to
     ravish (= rape) his friend's wife,
     Lucrece; the story is told in
     Shakespeare's narrative poem *The
     Rape of Lucrece*.
     design: aim.
56 *firm-set*: stable.
58 *prate*: blab, tell tales.
59 *take . . . time*: break this deadly
     silence which is so appropriate for the
     present moment.
61 *Words . . . gives*: the cold breath of
     words only cools down hot deeds.
63 *knell*: funeral bell rung to announce a
     death.

40 I see thee yet, in form as palpable
     As this which now I draw.
     Thou marshall'st me the way that I was going,
     And such an instrument I was to use.
     Mine eyes are made the fools o'th'other senses,
45 Or else worth all the rest. I see thee still,
     And on thy blade and dudgeon gouts of blood,
     Which was not so before. There's no such thing:
     It is the bloody business which informs
     Thus to mine eyes. Now o'er the one half-world
50 Nature seems dead, and wicked dreams abuse
     The curtain'd sleep. Witchcraft celebrates
     Pale Hecate's off'rings, and wither'd murder,
     Alarum'd by his sentinel, the wolf,
     Whose howl's his watch, thus with his stealthy pace,
55 With Tarquin's ravishing strides, towards his design
     Moves like a ghost. Thou sure and firm-set earth,
     Hear not my steps, which way they walk, for fear
     Thy very stones prate of my whereabout,
     And take the present horror from the time,
60 Which now suits with it. Whiles I threat, he lives;
     Words to the heat of deeds too cold breath gives.

     A bell rings

     I go, and it is done. The bell invites me.
     Hear it not, Duncan, for it is a knell
     That summons thee to heaven or to hell.   [*Exit*

Act 2 Scene 2
Duncan has been murdered. Macbeth is already regretting his action, and Lady Macbeth takes the daggers away from him.

1–2   *That . . . fire*: Like Duncan's two chamberlains, Lady Macbeth has been drinking.

3   *owl*: The owl (like the raven) was thought to be a bird of ill omen and is now compared to the night watchman who rings his bell outside the cells of prisoners condemned to death.
4   *the . . . night*: the last good-night. *about it*: doing the deed.
5   *surfeited grooms*: drunken servants.
6   *possets*: hot milky drinks with added liquor and spices, 'nightcaps'.
7–8   *death . . . die*: death and life are struggling to decide whether the attendants live or die.

9–13   *Alack . . . don't*: Lady Macbeth does not immediately see her husband—perhaps because he enters upstage behind her, or because the scene is in (imaginary) darkness.
10   *th'attempt*: the attempt to kill Duncan.
11   *confounds*: ruins.

15   *crickets*: The Elizabethans believed that the chirping of these insects was a herald of death.

Scene 2

Macbeth's castle; enter Lady Macbeth

Lady Macbeth
That which hath made them drunk, hath made me
    bold;
What hath quench'd them, hath given me fire.

An owl shrieks

                                Hark, peace!
It was the owl that shriek'd, the fatal bellman
Which gives the stern'st good-night. He is about it.
5 The doors are open, and the surfeited grooms
Do mock their charge with snores. I have drugg'd their
    possets,
That death and nature do contend about them,
Whether they live, or die.

Enter Macbeth *with two bloody daggers*

Macbeth
                  Who's there? What ho?
Lady Macbeth
Alack, I am afraid they have awak'd,
10 And 'tis not done; th'attempt and not the deed
Confounds us. Hark! I laid their daggers ready,
He could not miss 'em. Had he not resembled
My father as he slept, I had done't. My husband?
    Macbeth
I have done the deed. Didst thou not hear a noise?
    Lady Macbeth
15 I heard the owl scream and the crickets cry.
Did not you speak?
    Macbeth
When?
    Lady Macbeth
Now.

Macbeth

As I descended?

Lady Macbeth

20 Ay.

Macbeth

Hark, who lies i'th'second chamber?

Lady Macbeth

Donaldbain.

Macbeth

This is a sorry sight.

Lady Macbeth

A foolish thought, to say a sorry sight.

Macbeth

25 There's one did laugh in's sleep, and one cried
    'Murder!',

That they did wake each other; I stood, and heard
    them,

But they did say their prayers and address'd them

Again to sleep.

Lady Macbeth

                    There are two lodg'd together.

Macbeth

One cried 'God bless us!' and 'Amen' the other,

30 As they had seen me with these hangman's hands.

List'ning their fear, I could not say 'Amen'

When they did say 'God bless us.'

Lady Macbeth

Consider it not so deeply.

Macbeth

But wherefore could not I pronounce 'Amen'?

35 I had most need of blessing and 'Amen'

Stuck in my throat.

Lady Macbeth

                        These deeds must not be thought

After these ways; so, it will make us mad.

Macbeth

Methought I heard a voice cry, 'Sleep no more:

Macbeth does murder sleep', the innocent sleep,

40 Sleep that knits up the ravell'd sleeve of care,

The death of each day's life, sore labour's bath,

23 *a sorry sight*: a miserable sight;
   Macbeth is probably looking at his
   hands, which are holding the daggers.

27 *address'd them*: prepared themselves.
28 *lodg'd together*: sharing one bed (a
   common Elizabethan practice).
30 *As*: as if.
   hangman's hands: The hangman's
   duties included disembowelling the
   body of the hanged man.

36 *thought*: considered.

38 *Methought*: it seemed to me.

40 *ravell'd*: frayed; twisted.
   sleeve: part of garment; filament of
   silk (*sleave*).

42 *second course*: main dish (following
the 'starter').
48 *unbend*: slacken, weaken; the word
continues the metaphor started in
1, 7, 60 and 79.

50 *witness*: evidence.

58 *a painted devil*: the picture of a devil.
59–60 *gild . . . guilt*: Lady Macbeth
makes a cruel pun.
60s.d. *Knock within*: The offstage
knocking is the first sign that the
outside world is reacting (without yet
knowing it) to the crime that has been
committed.

61 *appals*: terrifies, dismays.
62 *they . . . eyes*: Macbeth's eyes seem to
be falling out of his head at the sight
of his bloody hands.

65 *multitudinous seas*: numerous oceans,
all the world's many seas.
incarnadine: stain red. See 'About the
Play', p.v.

Balm of hurt minds, great nature's second course,
Chief nourisher in life's feast.
Lady Macbeth
                                    What do you mean?
Macbeth
Still it cried, 'Sleep no more' to all the house;
45 'Glamis hath murder'd sleep', and therefore Cawdor
Shall sleep no more: Macbeth shall sleep no more.
Lady Macbeth
Who was it, that thus cried? Why, worthy thane,
You do unbend your noble strength to think
So brain-sickly of things. Go get some water
50 And wash this filthy witness from your hand.
Why did you bring these daggers from the place?
They must lie there. Go carry them and smear
The sleepy grooms with blood.
Macbeth
                                          I'll go no more.
I am afraid to think what I have done;
55 Look on't again, I dare not.
Lady Macbeth
                                    Infirm of purpose!
Give me the daggers. The sleeping and the dead
Are but as pictures; 'tis the eye of childhood
That fears a painted devil. If he do bleed,
I'll gild the faces of the grooms withal,
60 For it must seem their guilt.   [*Exit*

Knock within

Macbeth
                                    Whence is that knocking?
How is't with me, when every noise appals me?
What hands are here? Ha: they pluck out mine eyes.
Will all great Neptune's ocean wash this blood
Clean from my hand? No: this my hand will rather
65 The multitudinous seas incarnadine,
Making the green one red.

Enter Lady Macbeth

67 *I shame*: I would be ashamed.
68 *white*: bloodless.

Lady Macbeth
My hands are of your colour, but I shame
To wear a heart so white.

Knock within

I hear a knocking
At the south entry. Retire we to our chamber;
70 A little water clears us of this deed.
How easy is it then! Your constancy
Hath left you unattended.

71–2 *your . . . unattended*: your strength
of purpose has deserted you, you've
lost your nerve.

Knock within

Hark, more knocking.
Get on your night-gown, lest occasion call us
And show us to be watchers. Be not lost
75 So poorly in your thoughts.

73 *night-gown*: dressing-gown.
lest . . . us: in case there is need to
call for us.
74 *to be watchers*: to be awake.

Macbeth
To know my deed, 'twere best not know my self.

76 *To know . . . myself*: to recognize what
I have done it would be better if I
forgot who I am; as a murderer,
Macbeth will have a new identity.

Knock within

Wake Duncan with thy knocking: I would thou
couldst.   [*Exeunt*

'I pray you, remember the porter.'
(2, 3, 18–19) Adrian Schiller as the Porter,
Royal Shakespeare Company, 1996.

Act 2 Scene 3
All is discovered. The Porter is roused from
his drunken sleep by Macduff and Lennox,
who try to wake the king and find he has
been murdered. Macbeth panics, and kills
Duncan's attendants—and Duncan's sons,
afraid for their own safety, slip away
secretly.

1–2 *hell-gate*: the entrance to hell.
2 *old*: plenty of.
4 *Beelzebub*: A popular (biblical) name
for the devil.
4–19 *Here's . . . porter*: The Porter (a
part played by the company's chief
comic actor) introduces a selection of
imaginary characters as they come
through 'hell-gate'.
5 *plenty*: a good harvest (which would
bring down the price of corn).
8 *Faith*: by my faith (a mild oath).
8–11 *an equivocator . . . heaven*: The
Porter seems to be referring to the
Jesuit Father Garnet, who tried to save
his life with his specious arguments
but who was executed in 1606 for
complicity in the Gunpowder Plot: see
'Source, Date, and Text', p.xxvii.
9 *scales*: weighing-scales, scales of
justice.
10 *for God's sake*: A common oath, but
perhaps specifically referring to the
Jesuit priest's equivocal oaths.

SCENE 3

Macbeth's *castle*: *enter a* Porter. *Knocking within*

Porter
Here's a knocking indeed: if a man were porter of hell-
gate, he should have old turning the key. [*Knock*]
Knock, knock, knock. Who's there i'th'name of
Beelzebub? Here's a farmer that hanged himself on
th'expectation of plenty. Come in time—have napkins
enough about you, here you'll sweat for't. [*Knock*]
Knock, knock. Who's there in th'other devil's name?
Faith, here's an equivocator that could swear in both the
scales against either scale, who committed treason
enough for God's sake, yet could not equivocate to

12–13 *English tailor . . . French hose*:
English fashions often imitated the
French, and the tailor might have
been over-economical with fabric.

14 *roast your goose*: heat up your iron
('goose' = tailor's long-handled iron).

17 *primrose*: easy, attractive.
18 *Anon*: immediately, I'm coming.
19 *remember*: i.e. with a tip for opening
the gate.
22 *carousing*: celebrating, drinking.
till . . . cock: until the cock crowed for
a second time (i.e. about 3 a.m.).
23 *a great . . . things*: The Porter, hoping
for another tip, tries to engage the
callers in a riddle.
24 *What . . . provoke*: Macduff picks up
the cue and plays straight man to the
Porter.
25 *Marry*: an abbreviated form of the mild
oath 'By the Virgin Mary'.
nose-painting: making the nose red.
28 *equivocator*: double-dealer.
28–9 *makes . . . mars him*: rouses him to
sexual activity, then makes him
impotent.
31–2 *equivocates . . . sleep*: fulfils his
desire only in a dream.
32 *giving . . . lie*: cheating him; throwing
him down (as in wrestling); making
him lose his erection; forcing him to
urinate.
34 *i'the very throat*: utterly.
requited him: paid him back.
36 *took up my legs*: made me fall down.
shift: stratagem.
37 *cast him*: throw him to the ground,
vomit him up.

heaven. O, come in, equivocator. [*Knock*] Knock, knock, knock. Who's there? Faith, here's an English tailor come hither for stealing out of a French hose. Come in, tailor, here you may roast your goose. [*Knock*] Knock, knock.
15 Never at quiet: what are you? But this place is too cold for hell. I'll devil-porter it no further: I had thought to have let in some of all professions that go the primrose way to th'everlasting bonfire. [*Knock*] Anon, anon. I pray you, remember the porter. [*Opens door*]

Enter Macduff *and* Lennox

Macduff
20 Was it so late, friend, ere you went to bed,
That you do lie so late?
   Porter
Faith, sir, we were carousing till the second cock, and drink, sir, is a great provoker of three things.
   Macduff
What three things does drink especially provoke?
   Porter
25 Marry, sir, nose-painting, sleep, and urine. Lechery, sir, it provokes, and unprovokes: it provokes the desire, but it takes away the performance. Therefore much drink may be said to be an equivocator with lechery: it makes him, and it mars him; it sets him on, and it takes him
30 off; it persuades him and disheartens him, makes him stand to and not stand to. In conclusion, equivocates him in a sleep, and giving him the lie, leaves him.
   Macduff
I believe drink gave thee the lie last night.
   Porter
That it did, sir, i'the very throat on me, but I requited
35 him for his lie, and, I think, being too strong for him, though he took up my legs sometime, yet I made a shift to cast him.

37s.d. *Enter Macbeth*: The Porter's comedy has given the actor time to wash his hands and change costume.

38 *stirring*: awake.

Enter Macbeth

Macduff
Is thy master stirring?
Our knocking has awak'd him: here he comes.

[*Exit* Porter

Lennox
40 Good morrow, noble sir.
    Macbeth
                              Good morrow, both.

Macduff
Is the king stirring, worthy thane?
    Macbeth
                              Not yet.

Macduff
He did command me to call timely on him;
I have almost slipp'd the hour.
    Macbeth
                              I'll bring you to him.

Macduff
I know this is a joyful trouble to you, but yet 'tis one.
    Macbeth
45 The labour we delight in physics pain. This is the door.
    Macduff
I'll make so bold to call, for 'tis my limited service.

[*Exit*

Lennox
Goes the king hence today?
    Macbeth
He does—he did appoint so.
    Lennox
The night has been unruly: where we lay,
50 Our chimneys were blown down, and, as they say,
    Lamentings heard i'th'air, strange screams of death
    And prophesying with accents terrible
    Of dire combustion and confus'd events,
    New hatch'd to th'woeful time. The obscure bird
55 Clamour'd the livelong night. Some say, the earth
    Was feverous and did shake.
        Macbeth
                              'Twas a rough night.

42 *timely*: early.
43 *slipp'd the hour*: missed the time.

46 *limited*: appointed.

52 *prophesying*: people have been prophesying.
53–4 *dire . . . time*: terrible confusion and strange new happenings that have come out of this dreadful time; Lennox refers to the war with Norway—but his words have a more immediate application.
54 *The obscure bird*: the owl, which is usually seen and heard only at night.
55 *the livelong night*: throughout the whole long night.

57–8 *My . . . to it*: I can't remember a night like this in all my young life.

Lennox
My young remembrance cannot parallel
A fellow to it.

Enter Macduff

Macduff
O horror, horror, horror,
60 Tongue nor heart cannot conceive, nor name thee.
Macbeth and **Lennox**
What's the matter?
Macduff

62 *Confusion*: chaos.

63 *sacrilegious*: unholy.
ope: open.

64 *The . . . temple*: The king's body (which had been anointed with holy oil at his coronation, to signify that he was God's deputy on earth).

Confusion now hath made his masterpiece:
Most sacrilegious murder hath broke ope
The Lord's anointed temple and stole thence
65 The life o'th'building.
Macbeth
What is't you say, the life?
Lennox
Mean you his majesty?
Macduff

69 *a new Gorgon*: In Greek mythology the Gorgon Medusa, a monster with snakes for hair, turned every man to stone who looked on her; the sight of Duncan's murdered body will have the same effect.

73–4 *Shake . . . itself*: Macduff calls everybody to wake from sleep, which is only an imitation ('counterfeit') of death, to look on the real thing.

73 *downy*: soft, comfortable (because their pillows would be stuffed with 'down' = a bird's soft under-feathers).

74–5 *see . . . image*: see a sight like a picture of the Last Judgement (the 'great doom').

76 *As . . . sprites*: rise up like ghosts from their graves (and as the Christian dead will do at the Last Judgement).

77 *countenance*: come face to face with.

78 *trumpet*: alarum bell (perhaps sounding like the 'last trumpet' which will arouse the dead on Judgement Day—1 Corinthians 15:52).
parley: conference.

Approach the chamber and destroy your sight
With a new Gorgon. Do not bid me speak:
70 See and then speak yourselves.
[*Exeunt* Macbeth *and* Lennox
Awake, awake!
Ring the alarum bell! Murder and treason!
Banquo and Donaldbain! Malcolm, awake,
Shake off this downy sleep, death's counterfeit,
And look on death itself. Up, up, and see
75 The great doom's image. Malcolm, Banquo,
As from your graves rise up and walk like sprites
To countenance this horror.

Bell rings. Enter Lady Macbeth

Lady Macbeth
                                        What's the business
That such a hideous trumpet calls to parley
The sleepers of the house? Speak, speak.

Macduff

O gentle lady,

80 'Tis not for you to hear what I can speak.
The repetition in a woman's ear
Would murder as it fell.—

Enter Banquo

O Banquo, Banquo,
Our royal master's murder'd.
    Lady Macbeth

Woe, alas,

What, in our house?
    Banquo

Too cruel, anywhere.

85 Dear Duff, I prithee contradict thyself
And say it is not so.

Enter Macbeth *and* Lennox

Macbeth
Had I but died an hour before this chance,
I had liv'd a blessed time, for from this instant,
There's nothing serious in mortality.

90 All is but toys; renown and grace is dead,
The wine of life is drawn, and the mere lees
Is left this vault to brag of.

Enter Malcolm *and* Donaldbain

Donaldbain
What is amiss?
    Macbeth

You are, and do not know't,
The spring, the head, the fountain of your blood

95 Is stopp'd, the very source of it is stopp'd.
    Macduff
Your royal father's murder'd.
    Malcolm

O, by whom?

81–2 *The . . . fell*: to repeat this matter to a woman would kill her as the words fell from my mouth.

87 *before this chance*: before this happened.
88 *blessed*: blessèd.
89 *nothing . . . mortality*: nothing important in life.
90 *toys*: trivialities, rubbish.
91–2 *The wine . . . of*: Macbeth compares the earth to a wine-cellar ('vault') from which the best wine has been 'drawn' (= drained from the cask), so that now it can boast ('brag') only of the dregs ('lees').

98 *badg'd*: wearing the badges of their profession (as murderers).

100 *distracted*: confused.

103 *Wherefore*: why.

104 *temp'rate*: temperate, restrained.
106–7 *Th'expedition . . . reason*: in my passionate love, I didn't stop to think.
107 *pauser*: that which should make me hesitate.
108 *His . . . blood*: Macbeth's imagery seems to cover Duncan with a rich garment.
109–10 *his . . . entrance*: Duncan's wounds were like a break in the shoreline where the sea's destruction has broken in.
110–11 *the murderers . . . trade*: the murderers wearing the coloured uniforms of their trade: Macbeth develops the image that Lennox began in line 98.
111 *Steep'd*: dyed.
112 *Unmannerly breech'd*: improperly dressed, wearing indecent clothing.
gore: blood.
refrain: stop himself from acting.
114 *make's*: make his.
116–17 *that . . . ours*: when the matter concerns us more than anyone else.

117–19 *What . . . us*: what can we say here, where our own fate may be secretly hiding, ready to rush out and seize upon us.
118 *auger hole*: hole made with a sharp-pointed tool.
119 *brew'd*: ready to be poured out (i.e. like ale).
120 *upon . . . motion*: ready to move, ready to express itself.
122 *naked frailties*: bare bodies.

Lennox
Those of his chamber, as it seem'd, had done't.
Their hands and faces were all badg'd with blood,
So were their daggers which, unwip'd, we found
100 Upon their pillows. They star'd and were distracted;
No man's life was to be trusted with them.
Macbeth
O, yet I do repent me of my fury
That I did kill them.
Macduff
                                        Wherefore did you so?
Macbeth
Who can be wise, amaz'd, temp'rate, and furious,
105 Loyal and neutral, in a moment? No man.
Th'expedition of my violent love
Outran the pauser, reason. Here lay Duncan,
His silver skin lac'd with his golden blood
And his gash'd stabs look'd like a breach in nature,
110 For ruin's wasteful entrance. There the murderers,
Steep'd in the colours of their trade; their daggers
Unmannerly breech'd with gore. Who could refrain,
That had a heart to love and in that heart
Courage to make's love known?
Lady Macbeth
                                        Help me hence, ho.
Macduff
115 Look to the lady.   [*Exit* Lady Macbeth, *helped*
Malcolm
[*To* Donaldbain] Why do we hold our tongues, that most may claim
This argument for ours?
Donaldbain
[*To* Malcolm]   What should be spoken here,
Where our fate hid in an auger hole may rush
And seize us? Let's away. Our tears are not yet brew'd.
Malcolm
120 [*To* Donaldbain] Nor our strong sorrow upon the foot
of motion.
Banquo
Look to the lady,
And when we have our naked frailties hid

126 *In . . . God*: under God's great
protection.
127 *undivulg'd pretence*: unrevealed claim
(to the crown).

129 *manly readiness*: everyday garments
(instead of the 'night-gown' advised by
Lady Macbeth in *2, 2, 73*).

131 *consort*: associate.

132–3 *To show . . . easy*: a hypocrite can
easily show a sorrow that he doesn't
feel.

134–5 *Our separated . . . safer*: we'll both
be safer if we keep apart.

136–7 *the nea'er . . . bloody*: the more
closely related (to Duncan), the more
likely to be killed.

138 *lighted*: landed, found its target.

140 *be . . . leave-taking*: make a fuss
about saying a formal goodbye.
141 *shift*: get away quietly.
141–2 *there's . . . left*: it's an authorized
theft, to steal (oneself) away from a
place where there is no mercy:
Malcolm closes the scene with a
rhyme and a grim pun.

That suffer in exposure, let us meet
And question this most bloody piece of work
125 To know it further. Fears and scruples shake us:
In the great hand of God I stand and thence
Against the undivulg'd pretence I fight
Of treasonous malice.
    Macduff
               And so do I.
    All
                     So all.
    Macbeth
Let's briefly put on manly readiness
130 And meet i'th'hall together.
    All
                  Well contented.
        [Exeunt all but Malcolm *and* Donaldbain
    Malcolm
What will you do? Let's not consort with them.
To show an unfelt sorrow is an office
Which the false man does easy. I'll to England.
    Donaldbain
To Ireland, I. Our separated fortune
135 Shall keep us both the safer. Where we are,
There's daggers in men's smiles; the nea'er in blood,
The nearer bloody.
    Malcolm
             This murderous shaft that's shot
Hath not yet lighted, and our safest way
Is to avoid the aim. Therefore to horse,
140 And let us not be dainty of leave-taking,
But shift away. There's warrant in that theft
Which steals itself when there's no mercy left.
                     [Exeunt

Act 2 Scene 4

Ross and an Old Man discuss the unnatural events that occurred on the night of Duncan's murder. They learn from Macduff that the king's two sons have fled, and that Macbeth has been chosen to be the next king.

1 *Old Man*: This unnamed character speaks for the common man who is affected by the situation but not involved in the action.

3 *sore*: severe, harsh.

4 *trifled former knowings*: made the things I knew before seem trivial.
father: A title of respect.

5–6 *the heavens . . . stage*: In Shakespeare's day it was generally believed that events in the greater world of nature (the 'macrocosm') reflected, or were affected by, events in the little world of man (the 'microcosm').

5 *act*: deed; performance.

6 *his bloody stage*: the scene of his bloodthirsty performance.

7 *travelling lamp*: the sun.

8 *predominance*: superior influence.

9 *entomb*: bury.

12 *pride of place*: the highest point of flight.

13 *mousing*: mouse-hunting.
hawk'd at: snatched up on the wing (as a hawk takes its prey).

15 *minions of their race*: best of their breed.

16 *broke their stalls*: broke out of their stables.

17 *Contending 'gainst obedience*: rebelling against the training that had made them obedient.

18 *eat*: ate.

Scene 4

Somewhere in Scotland: enter Ross, *with an* Old Man

Old Man
Threescore and ten I can remember well;
Within the volume of which time, I have seen
Hours dreadful and things strange, but this sore night
Hath trifled former knowings.
　Ross
　　　　　　　　Ha, good father,
5 Thou seest the heavens, as troubled with man's act,
Threatens his bloody stage. By th'clock 'tis day
And yet dark night strangles the travelling lamp.
Is't night's predominance, or the day's shame,
That darkness does the face of earth entomb
10 When living light should kiss it?
　Old Man
　　　　　　　　　　'Tis unnatural,
Even like the deed that's done. On Tuesday last,
A falcon tow'ring in her pride of place
Was by a mousing owl hawk'd at and kill'd.
　Ross
And Duncan's horses, a thing most strange and certain,
15 Beauteous and swift, the minions of their race,
Turn'd wild in nature, broke their stalls, flung out,
Contending 'gainst obedience as they would
Make war with mankind.
　Old Man
　　　　　　　　'Tis said, they eat each other.

Ross
They did so, to th'amazement of mine eyes
20 That looked upon't.

Enter Macduff

                        Here comes the good Macduff.
How goes the world, sir, now?
    Macduff
                        Why, see you not?
    Ross
Is't known who did this more than bloody deed?
    Macduff
Those that Macbeth hath slain.
    Ross
                        Alas the day,
What good could they pretend?
    Macduff
                        They were suborn'd.
25 Malcolm and Donaldbain, the king's two sons,
Are stol'n away and fled, which puts upon them
Suspicion of the deed.
    Ross
                        'Gainst nature still.
Thriftless ambition that will ravin up
Thine own life's means. Then 'tis most like
30 The sovereignty will fall upon Macbeth.
    Macduff
He is already nam'd and gone to Scone
To be invested.
    Ross
Where is Duncan's body?
    Macduff
                        Carried to Colmkill,
The sacred storehouse of his predecessors
35 And guardian of their bones.
    Ross
                        Will you to Scone?
    Macduff
No, cousin, I'll to Fife.

19–20 *They . . . upon't:* Ross confirms the rumour with the evidence of his own eyes.

24 *What . . . pretend:* what good did they think it would do for them.
suborn'd: bribed.

27 *'Gainst nature still:* like all those other unnatural happenings.
28 *Thriftless:* wasteful.
ravin up: devour.
29 *Thine . . . means:* that which was necessary to give you life.

31 *nam'd:* chosen.
Scone: Once the capital of Scotland, and the traditional site of Scottish coronations.
32 *invested:* installed ceremonially.

33 *Colmkill:* the island of Iona.

36 *Fife:* Macduff's ancestral home.
will thither: will go there.

Ross

                Well, I will thither.

Macduff

Well may you see things well done there. Adieu,
Lest our old robes sit easier than our new.

Ross

Farewell, father.

Old Man

40 God's benison go with you, and with those
That would make good of bad, and friends of foes.

                                    [*Exeunt*

40 *benison*: blessing.

ACT 3

Act 3 Scene 1
Banquo is suspicious—and Macbeth
arranges to have him murdered.

SCENE 1

Macbeth's castle: enter Banquo *dressed for riding*

Banquo
Thou hast it now, King, Cawdor, Glamis, all,
As the weïrd women promis'd, and I fear
Thou played'st most foully for't; yet it was said
It should not stand in thy posterity,
5 But that myself should be the root and father
Of many kings. If there come truth from them—
As upon thee, Macbeth, their speeches shine—
Why by the verities on thee made good,
May they not be my oracles as well
10 And set me up in hope? But hush, no more.

Sennet sounded. Enter Macbeth *as King,* Lady
Macbeth *as Queen,* Lennox, Ross, Lords, *and*
Attendants

Macbeth
Here's our chief guest.
Lady Macbeth
                              If he had been forgotten,
It had been as a gap in our great feast
And all thing unbecoming.
Macbeth
Tonight we hold a solemn supper, sir,
15 And I'll request your presence.
Banquo
                              Let your highness
Command upon me, to the which my duties
Are with a most indissoluble tie
Forever knit.
Macbeth
Ride you this afternoon?

---

2 *weïrd*: mystic, supernatural.

4 *stand . . . posterity*: be inherited by
your descendants.
5–6 *father . . . kings*: According to
popular legend, King James was one
of Banquo's descendants.
7 *shine*: look favourably.
8 *verities . . . good*: prophecies that
have come true in your case.

10s.d. *Sennet*: A distinctive set of
musical notes played on trumpet to
herald a specific individual, (like a
modern signature tune).

13 *all thing unbecoming*: quite improper.

14 *solemn supper*: formal dinner.

16 *to the which*: to which command.
17–18 *with . . . knit*: bound with a tie
that cannot be broken.

19 *Ride . . . afternoon*: Macbeth is
beginning to lay his plans.

22 *still*: always.
    grave and prosperous: serious and
    profitable.
23 *council*: i.e. meeting of the Privy
    Council.

26–8 *Go not . . . twain*: if my horse won't
    go any faster, I shall have to take up
    one or two ('twain') hours of darkness.

31 *bloody*: stained with the blood of
    Duncan.
    are bestow'd: have taken refuge.
33 *parricide*: murder of their father.
34 *invention*: tales they have invented.
34–6 *of that . . . jointly*: we will talk
    about that tomorrow, when there will
    also be affairs of state that demand
    our joint attention.

38 *our time . . . upon's*: we're in rather a
    hurry.

42 *master of his time*: be free to do as he
    wants.

46 *Sirrah*: A condescending form of
    address to a social inferior.

48 *without*: outside.

Banquo
20 Ay, my good lord.
    Macbeth
    We should have else desir'd your good advice
    Which still hath been both grave and prosperous
    In this day's council: but we'll take tomorrow.
    Is't far you ride?
    Banquo
25 As far, my lord, as will fill up the time
    'Twixt this and supper. Go not my horse the better,
    I must become a borrower of the night
    For a dark hour, or twain.
    Macbeth
    Fail not our feast.
    Banquo
30 My lord, I will not.
    Macbeth
    We hear our bloody cousins are bestow'd
    In England and in Ireland, not confessing
    Their cruel parricide, filling their hearers
    With strange invention. But of that tomorrow,
35 When therewithal we shall have cause of state
    Craving us jointly. Hie you to horse; adieu,
    Till you return at night. Goes Fleance with you?
    Banquo
    Ay, my good lord; our time does call upon's.
    Macbeth
    I wish your horses swift and sure of foot,
40 And so I do commend you to their backs.
    Farewell.   [*Exit* Banquo
    Let every man be master of his time
    Till seven at night; to make society
    The sweeter welcome, we will keep ourself
45 Till supper-time alone. While then, God be with you.
                        [*Exeunt all but* Macbeth *and a* Servant
    Sirrah, a word with you: attend those men
    Our pleasure?
    Servant
    They are, my lord, without the palace gate.
    Macbeth
    Bring them before us.   [*Exit* Servant

49–50 *To be . . . thus*: it is nothing to be king as I am now—I must be king in safety.

51 *stick deep*: are deeply rooted.

51–2 *in his . . . fear'd*: there's something overpowering in his natural nobility of character that I should be afraid of.

53 *to . . . temper*: in addition to that courageous spirit.

56–8 *under. . . Caesar*: Mark Antony was told by a soothsayer that his guiding spirit ('genius') was not powerful enough to oppose that of Octavius Caesar (see *Antony and Cleopatra*, 2, 3, 20–3).

58 *chid*: chided, reproved.

62–3 *Upon . . . gripe*: put a crown on my head and a sceptre in my hand ('gripe' = grasp) that could not be passed on to my descendants.

64 *unlineal hand*: not in my line of descent, not descended from me.

66 *issue*: descendants.
fil'd: defiled.

68 *rancours*: bitter ill-feelings.
vessel: drinking-vessel, chalice.

69 *eternal jewel*: immortal soul.

70 *common . . . man*: i.e. the devil (who is the enemy of everybody).

72 *come . . . list*: let Fate come into combat like a medieval knight into the tournament.

73 *champion . . . utterance*: challenge me to deadly combat.

77–92 *Well then . . . forever*: Macbeth begins to speak in prose, to win the Murderers' confidence.

78 *he*: i.e. Banquo.

79 *under fortune*: below what you deserved.

80 *made good*: explained.

81 *passed in probation*: proved, demonstrated.

82 *borne in hand*: deceived, deliberately misled.
crossed: frustrated.
the instruments: the means that were used.

83 *wrought*: worked.

To be thus is nothing,
50 But to be safely thus. Our fears in Banquo
Stick deep, and in his royalty of nature
Reigns that which would be fear'd. 'Tis much he dares,
And to that dauntless temper of his mind,
He hath a wisdom that doth guide his valour
55 To act in safety. There is none but he,
Whose being I do fear; and under him
My genius is rebuk'd, as it is said
Mark Antony's was by Caesar. He chid the sisters
When first they put the name of king upon me
60 And bade them speak to him. Then prophet-like,
They hail'd him father to a line of kings.
Upon my head they plac'd a fruitless crown
And put a barren sceptre in my gripe,
Thence to be wrench'd with an unlineal hand,
65 No son of mine succeeding. If't be so,
For Banquo's issue have I fil'd my mind;
For them, the gracious Duncan have I murder'd,
Put rancours in the vessel of my peace
Only for them, and mine eternal jewel
70 Given to the common enemy of man,
To make them kings, the seeds of Banquo kings.
Rather than so, come Fate into the list,
And champion me to th'utterance. Who's there?

Enter Servant *and two* Murderers

[*To* Servant] Now go to the door and stay there till we
      call.   [*Exit* Servant
75 Was it not yesterday we spoke together?
  Murderers
It was, so please your highness.
  Macbeth
Well then, now have you considered of my speeches?
Know, that it was he in the times past which held you so
under fortune, which you thought had been our
80 innocent self. This I made good to you in our last
conference; passed in probation with you how you were
borne in hand, how crossed; the instruments, who
wrought with them, and all things else that might to

84 *soul*: mind.
 notion: intellect.

90 *gospelled*: influenced by the teaching
 of the Christian Gospels ('Love your
 enemies, bless them that curse you,
 do good to them that hate you, and
 pray for them which despitefully use
 you, and persecute you', Matthew
 5:44).

94–103 *in the catalogue . . . men*: you
 are classified as 'men' in any general
 list of creatures, just as different
 breeds of dog are all included under
 'dogs'; but a more valuable listing is
 that which notes the precise qualities
 of the animals, according to their
 natural abilities; this list, where the
 dog receives individual description
 ('Particular addition'), is distinct from
 the inventory ('bill') that counts them
 all alike. The same is true of men.

96 *Shoughs*: a kind of lap-dog.
 water-rugs: probably a kind of long-
 haired retriever useful in water.
 demi-wolves: cross-breeds, half wolf
 and half dog.
 clept: called.

99 *housekeeper*: domestic guard dog.

104 *station*: position, rank.

106–7 *I will . . . off*: I will tell you secretly
 ('in your bosoms') of a plan which,
 when it is carried out, removes your
 enemy.

108 *Grapples . . . us*: fastens you firmly to
 my affections (as grappling-irons hold
 fighting ships together in battle).

109–10 *Who . . . perfect*: Macbeth will
 feel ill as long as Banquo is alive, but
 he would be perfectly healthy if
 Banquo were dead.

109 *wear*: Macbeth continues to use
 clothing metaphors.

115 *set . . . chance*: gamble my life on
 anything.

half a soul and to a notion crazed say, 'Thus did
85 Banquo.'

First Murderer
You made it known to us.

Macbeth
I did so, and went further, which is now our point of
second meeting. Do you find your patience so
predominant in your nature, that you can let this go?
90 Are you so gospelled, to pray for this good man and for
his issue, whose heavy hand hath bowed you to the
grave and beggared yours forever?

First Murderer
We are men, my liege.

Macbeth
Ay, in the catalogue ye go for men,
95 As hounds, and greyhounds, mongrels, spaniels, curs,
Shoughs, water-rugs, and demi-wolves are clept
All by the name of dogs. The valu'd file
Distinguishes the swift, the slow, the subtle,
The housekeeper, the hunter, every one
100 According to the gift which bounteous nature
Hath in him clos'd, whereby he does receive
Particular addition from the bill
That writes them all alike. And so of men.
Now, if you have a station in the file
105 Not i'th'worst rank of manhood, say't,
And I will put that business in your bosoms,
Whose execution takes your enemy off,
Grapples you to the heart and love of us
Who wear our health but sickly in his life,
110 Which in his death were perfect.

Second Murderer
                                          I am one, my liege,
Whom the vile blows and buffets of the world
Hath so incens'd that I am reckless what I do
To spite the world.

First Murderer
                    And I another,
So weary with disasters, tugg'd with fortune,
115 That I would set my life on any chance
To mend it or be rid on't.

Macbeth

Both of you know
Banquo was your enemy.

Murderers

True, my lord.

Macbeth

So is he mine, and in such bloody distance
That every minute of his being thrusts
120 Against my near'st of life; and though I could
With barefac'd power sweep him from my sight
And bid my will avouch it, yet I must not,
For certain friends that are both his and mine,
Whose loves I may not drop, but wail his fall
125 Who I myself struck down. And thence it is
That I to your assistance do make love,
Masking the business from the common eye
For sundry weighty reasons.

Second Murderer

We shall, my lord,
Perform what you command us.

First Murderer

Though our lives—

Macbeth

130 Your spirits shine through you. Within this hour at
most,
I will advise you where to plant yourselves,
Acquaint you with the perfect spy o'th'time,
The moment on't, for't must be done tonight,
And something from the palace: always thought,
135 That I require a clearness. And with him,
To leave no rubs nor botches in the work,
Fleance, his son that keeps him company,
Whose absence is no less material to me
Than is his father's, must embrace the fate
140 Of that dark hour. Resolve yourselves apart,
I'll come to you anon.

Murderers

We are resolv'd, my lord.

118 *distance*: dissension.
119 *thrusts*: i.e. like a fencer's sword.
120 *near'st of life*: very existence, vital organs.
120–2 *though . . . avouch it*: although I have the power to kill him without giving any excuse, and say I did it just because I wanted to.
123 *For*: for the sake of.
124 *but wail*: but I must lament.

132 *perfect spy o'th'time*: best time I can see for the murder.
134 *something*: some distance.
thought: remembered.
135 *a clearness*: to be kept in the clear, to be free from all suspicion.
136 *rubs*: mistakes, impediments.
botches: bungling.
138 *Whose . . . to me*: whose death is just as important to me.
140 *Resolve . . . apart*: make up your minds about it (i.e. the additional murder of Fleance) in private.

142 *straight*: immediately.

Lady Macbeth is also uneasy; Macbeth
assures her that he will take some action—
but he refuses to tell her more.

3–4 *I would . . . words*: I would like to
have a few words with him when he
has time.
4–5 *Nought's had . . . content*: we have
gained nothing and lost everything
when we are not satisfied with what
we have got.
6–7 *'Tis safer . . . joy*: it is better to be
the one who is killed than to live in
such insecurity because we have
killed him.
10–11 *Using . . . on*: living with those
thoughts that should have died when
the subject of them (i.e. Duncan) was
killed.
13–15 *We have . . . tooth*: In killing
Duncan, Macbeth has only been
partially successful: the royal dynasty,
like a wounded snake, will recover,
and Macbeth's feeble violence ('poor
malice') will be again in danger of
reprisals from its power. Macbeth may
be speaking here as a king (using the
'royal plural'), or as a husband
(including Lady Macbeth in the
action).
13 *scorch'd*: notched, scored.
13–14 *snake . . . herself*: Although the
'snake' represents Duncan and his
male heirs, Macbeth still thinks of it
as female.

14 *close*: rejoin, heal up.
15 *tooth*: power.
16 *frame of things*: structure of the entire
universe.
both the worlds: earth and heaven.

Macbeth
I'll call upon you straight; abide within.

[*Exeunt* Murderers

It is concluded. Banquo, thy soul's flight,
If it find heaven, must find it out tonight.   [*Exit*

SCENE 2

Macbeth's castle: *enter* Lady Macbeth, *and a* Servant

Lady Macbeth
Is Banquo gone from court?
        Servant
Ay, madam, but returns again tonight.
        Lady Macbeth
Say to the king, I would attend his leisure
For a few words.
        Servant
                Madam, I will.   [*Exit*
        Lady Macbeth
                        Nought's had, all's spent
5 Where our desire is got without content.
   'Tis safer to be that which we destroy
   Than by destruction dwell in doubtful joy.

        Enter Macbeth

   How now, my lord, why do you keep alone,
   Of sorriest fancies your companions making,
10 Using those thoughts which should indeed have died
   With them they think on? Things without all remedy
   Should be without regard; what's done, is done.
        Macbeth
   We have scorch'd the snake, not kill'd it;
   She'll close, and be herself, whilst our poor malice
15 Remains in danger of her former tooth.
   But let the frame of things disjoint, both the worlds
        suffer,
   Ere we will eat our meal in fear, and sleep
   In the affliction of these terrible dreams
   That shake us nightly. Better be with the dead

25 *domestic*: at home, in Scotland.
foreign levy: armies gathered (levied) abroad.
27 *Gentle my lord*: my gentle lord.
28 *sleek o'er*: smooth down.
30 *remembrance*: regard, thought.
31 *present him eminence*: treat him with the highest respect.
32–3 *unsafe . . . streams*: in this insecure time we must wash ('lave') our royal titles in floods of flattery (to make them appear honourable).
34 *vizards*: masks; the part of helmet that covers the face.

38 *in them . . . eterne*: they are not immortal; Nature (or Life) does not hold an eternal copyright on Banquo and Fleance.
eterne: eternal.
39 *are assailable*: can be assaulted, attacked.
40 *jocund*: merry.
41 *cloister'd flight*: flight around the cloisters (= covered walks with open sides).
41–3 *ere . . . peal*: before the dung-beetle responds to the call of darkness, humming like an evening curfew-bell to call yawning people to sleep.
41 *black Hecate*: goddess of witchcraft.
42 *shard-born*: born in dung; an alternative spelling 'borne' permits a different meaning—'carried aloft by its wing-cases'.
45 *chuck*: chick (a term of endearment still used in England in parts of the Midlands).
46 *seeling*: stitching up; in falconry this refers to the sewing together of a young bird's eyelids for the purpose of training.
47 *Scarf up*: blindfold (as with a scarf over the eyes).

20 Whom we, to gain our peace, have sent to peace,
Than on the torture of the mind to lie
In restless ecstasy. Duncan is in his grave.
After life's fitful fever, he sleeps well;
Treason has done his worst; nor steel nor poison,
25 Malice domestic, foreign levy, nothing
Can touch him further.

Lady Macbeth
Come on. Gentle my lord,
Sleek o'er your rugged looks, be bright and jovial
Among your guests tonight.

Macbeth
                                        So shall I, love,
30 And so I pray be you. Let your remembrance
Apply to Banquo, present him eminence
Both with eye and tongue; unsafe the while, that we
Must lave our honours in these flattering streams
And make our faces vizards to our hearts,
35 Disguising what they are.

Lady Macbeth
                                        You must leave this.

Macbeth
O, full of scorpions is my mind, dear wife!
Thou know'st that Banquo and his Fleance lives.

Lady Macbeth
But in them Nature's copy's not eterne.

Macbeth
There's comfort yet, they are assailable;
40 Then be thou jocund: ere the bat hath flown
His cloister'd flight, ere to black Hecate's summons
The shard-born beetle with his drowsy hums
Hath rung night's yawning peal, there shall be done
A deed of dreadful note.

Lady Macbeth
                                        What's to be done?

Macbeth
45 Be innocent of the knowledge, dearest chuck,
Till thou applaud the deed. Come, seeling night,
Scarf up the tender eye of pitiful day
And with thy bloody and invisible hand

49 *Cancel . . . bond*: put an end to the
   lives of Banquo and Fleance; from a
   pun on 'seeling'/'sealing', Macbeth
   has led to the metaphor of a legal
   contract.

50 *keeps me pale*: restrains me; the
   'pale' was the boundary dividing one
   country's territory from the next.
   Light thickens: it's getting dark.

51 *rooky*: filled with rooks; crows and
   rooks, both black birds, are almost
   identical.

53 *night's black . . . rouse*: wicked
   creatures that work by night are
   waking up to hunt their prey.

54 *hold thee still*: carry on as you have
   been doing.

55 *Things . . . ill*: deeds that begin with
   evil grow stronger with more evil.

Cancel and tear to pieces that great bond
50 Which keeps me pale. Light thickens,
   And the crow makes wing to th'rooky wood;
   Good things of day begin to droop and drowse,
   Whiles night's black agents to their preys do rouse.
   Thou marvell'st at my words, but hold thee still;
55 Things bad begun, make strong themselves by ill.
   So prithee, go with me.   [*Exeunt*

Act 3 Scene 3
Banquo is murdered—but Fleance escapes.

1 *Third Murderer*: Perhaps Macbeth
  cannot trust even the Murderers he
  has chosen.

2 *He . . . mistrust*: there's no need for
  him to mistrust us.

3 *offices*: duties; see '*Macbeth*: the
  source', p.101.

4 *just*: exactly.

6 *lated*: belated.

7 *To . . . inn*: to get to the inn in time
  (before dark).

Scene 3

Some distance from Macbeth*'s castle: enter three*
Murderers

First Murderer
But who did bid thee join with us?
   Third Murderer
                                Macbeth.
   Second Murderer
He needs not our mistrust, since he delivers
Our offices and what we have to do
To the direction just.
   First Murderer
[*To* Third Murderer] Then stand with us.
5 The west yet glimmers with some streaks of day;
   Now spurs the lated traveller apace
   To gain the timely inn, and near approaches
   The subject of our watch.
   Third Murderer
                                Hark, I hear horses.
   Banquo
[*Within*] Give us a light there, ho!

Second Murderer

Then 'tis he; the rest

10 That are within the note of expectation

Already are i'th'court.

First Murderer

His horses go about.

Third Murderer

Almost a mile; but he does usually,

So all men do, from hence to th'palace gate

Make it their walk.

Enter Banquo *and* Fleance, *with a torch*

Second Murderer

15 A light, a light!

Third Murderer

'Tis he.

First Murderer

Stand to't.

Banquo

It will be rain tonight.

First Murderer

Let it come down.

The Murderers *attack.* First Murderer *strikes out the light*

Banquo

O, treachery!

20 Fly, good Fleance, fly, fly, fly!

Thou mayst revenge—O slave!

Dies. Fleance *escapes*

Third Murderer

Who did strike out the light?

First Murderer

Was't not the way?

Third Murderer

There's but one down; the son is fled.

9–10 *the rest . . . expectation*: the other expected guests.

11 *go about*: are going a long way round.

14 *Make . . . walk*: After a long journey the horses would be sweating, and it would be necessary for grooms to walk with them until they were cool.

Second Murderer
We have lost best half of our affair.
    First Murderer
25 Well, let's away, and say how much is done.

                      [*Exeunt, with* Banquo *'s body*

SCENE 4

*The Banqueting Hall. Banquet prepared. Two thrones
are placed on stage. Enter* Macbeth *as King,* Lady
Macbeth *as Queen,* Ross, Lennox, Lords, *and*
Attendants. Lady Macbeth *sits*

Macbeth
You know your own degrees, sit down; at first and last,
the hearty welcome.

The Lords *sit*

Lords
Thanks to your majesty.
    Macbeth
Our self will mingle with society and play the humble
5 host; our hostess keeps her state, but in best time we will
require her welcome.
    Lady Macbeth
Pronounce it for me, sir, to all our friends, for my heart
speaks they are welcome.

Enter First Murderer

    Macbeth
See, they encounter thee with their hearts' thanks.
10 Both sides are even; here I'll sit i'th'midst.
Be large in mirth, anon we'll drink a measure
The table round. [*To* First Murderer] There's blood
upon thy face.
    First Murderer
'Tis Banquo's then.

Act 3 Scene 4
Macbeth and his wife welcome the guests to their state banquet. The Ghost of Banquo appears but only Macbeth can see it, and his strange behaviour startles his wife and their guests.

0s.d. *Banquet prepared*: This might be an elaborate arrangement of fruit and sweets with wine, or else a full state dinner.
1 *degrees*: social ranks (which would determine the seating-order).
at first and last: to one and all.

5 *keeps her state*: remains seated on the throne of state.

9 *encounter*: respond to.
10 *Both . . . even*: there are equal numbers of people on both sides of the table.
11 *large*: unrestrained.
11–12 *drink . . . round*: drink a toast with each person around the table.

Macbeth
'Tis better thee without, than he within.
15 Is he dispatch'd?
  First Murderer
My lord, his throat is cut; that I did for him.
  Macbeth
Thou art the best o'th'cut-throats,
Yet he's good that did the like for Fleance;
If thou didst it, thou are the nonpareil.
  First Murderer
20 Most royal sir, Fleance is scap'd.
  Macbeth
Then comes my fit again: I had else been perfect;
Whole as the marble, founded as the rock,
As broad and general as the casing air:
But now I am cabin'd, cribb'd, confin'd, bound in
25 To saucy doubts and fears. But Banquo's safe?
  First Murderer
Ay, my good lord: safe in a ditch he bides,
With twenty trenched gashes on his head,
The least a death to nature.
  Macbeth   Thanks for that.
There the grown serpent lies; the worm that's fled
30 Hath nature that in time will venom breed,
No teeth for th'present. Get thee gone; tomorrow
We'll hear ourselves again.   [*Exit* First Murderer
  Lady Macbeth
                                      My royal lord,
You do not give the cheer; the feast is sold
That is not often vouch'd while 'tis a-making,
35 'Tis given with welcome. To feed were best at home:
From thence, the sauce to meat is ceremony,
Meeting were bare without it.

15 *dispatch'd*: dealt with—i.e. killed.

18 *the like*: the same.
19 *the nonpareil*: the best, without equal.

20 *scap'd*: escaped.

21 *fit*: spasm of fear.
   perfect: completely safe.
22 *Whole . . . rock*: solid as marble, firm as a rock.
23 *broad . . . air*: free and unconfined as the air surrounding us.
24 *cabin'd*: cramped into a small space.
   cribb'd: shut up in a stall.
25 *saucy*: intrusive, distracting.

27 *trenched*: trenchèd; hacked out.

28 *The least . . . nature*: even the smallest would kill a man.

29 *worm*: grub.

30–1 *nature . . . present*: will become poisonous in the natural course of things, but is harmless at present.

33 *give the cheer*: entertain your guests.
33–5 *the feast . . . welcome*: a banquet is no better than a meal that has to be paid for unless, during the feasting ('while 'tis a-making'), the guests are often told how welcome they are.
35–6 *to feed . . . ceremony*: it's better to eat at home, but the social rituals of a formal occasion add an extra sauce to a meal eaten away from home.
37 *Meeting . . . it*: a gathering of people needs these social rituals of courtesy.

Enter the Ghost of Banquo *and sits in* Macbeth's place

Macbeth
                              Sweet remembrancer!
Now good digestion wait on appetite,
And health on both.
          Lennox
                              May't please your highness, sit.
          Macbeth

40   Here had we now our country's honour roof'd,
Were the grac'd person of our Banquo present,
Who may I rather challenge for unkindness
Than pity for mischance.
          Ross
                              His absence, sir,
Lays blame upon his promise. Please't your highness
45   To grace us with your royal company?
          Macbeth
The table's full.
          Lennox
                              Here is a place reserv'd, sir.
          Macbeth
Where?
          Lennox
Here, my good lord. What is't that moves your
          highness?
          Macbeth
Which of you have done this?
          Lords
                              What, my good lord?
          Macbeth
50   Thou canst not say I did it; never shake
Thy gory locks at me!

40 *our . . . roof'd*: the nobility of our country complete (as a house is completed when the roof is put on).
42 *challenge for unkindness*: rebuke for lack of courtesy.
43 *pity for mischance*: be sorry for any accident that has happened to him.
43–4 *His absence . . . promise*: if he can't be here, he should not have promised to come.
44 *Please't*: may it please.

47 *Where?*: Only Macbeth can see the Ghost.

48 *moves*: distresses.

'Never shake Thy gory locks at me!' (*3*, 4, 50–1) Bob Peck as Macbeth, Royal Shakespeare Company, 1982.

Ross
Gentlemen, rise, his highness is not well.

Lady Macbeth *joins the* Lords

Lady Macbeth
Sit, worthy friends. My lord is often thus,
And hath been from his youth. Pray you, keep seat.
55 The fit is momentary; upon a thought
He will again be well. If much you note him
You shall offend him and extend his passion.
Feed, and regard him not. [*To* Macbeth] Are you a
man?

55 *upon a thought*: as fast as you can think it.
56 *note*: take notice of.

Macbeth
Ay, and a bold one, that dare look on that
60 Which might appal the devil.
    Lady Macbeth
                                O proper stuff!
This is the very painting of your fear;
This is the air-drawn dagger which you said
Led you to Duncan. O, these flaws and starts,
Impostors to true fear, would well become
65 A woman's story at a winter's fire
Authoriz'd by her grandam. Shame itself!
Why do you make such faces? When all's done
You look but on a stool.
    Macbeth
Prithee, see there! Behold, look, lo! How say you?
70 [*To* Ghost] Why, what care I? If thou canst nod, speak
    too.
If charnel-houses and our graves must send
Those that we bury back, our monuments
Shall be the maws of kites.   [*Exit* Ghost of Banquo
    Lady Macbeth
                                What, quite unmann'd in folly?
    Macbeth
If I stand here, I saw him.
    Lady Macbeth
                                Fie, for shame.
    Macbeth
75 Blood hath been shed ere now, i'th'olden time,
Ere humane statute purg'd the gentle weal;
Ay, and since too, murders have been perform'd
Too terrible for the ear. The time has been
That when the brains were out, the man would die,
80 And there an end. But now they rise again
With twenty mortal murders on their crowns
And push us from our stools. This is more strange
Than such a murder is.
    Lady Macbeth
                                My worthy lord,
Your noble friends do lack you.

60 *proper stuff*: absolute rubbish.
61 *painting*: image, imagination.
62 *air-drawn*: drawn in the air.
63 *flaws*: bursts of passion.
   starts: startled movements.
64 *Impostors to*: false imitations of.
65–6 *A woman's . . . grandam*: an old
   wife's tale for a winter evening round
   the fireside.
66 *grandam*: grandmother.
68 *stool*: The usual seating for
   Elizabethans; chairs were expensive
   and rare.

71–3 *If . . . back*: if vaults and graves
   can send back the bodies we have
   interred in them, our only burying-
   places will be the stomachs ('maws')
   of carrion-eating birds.
71 *charnel-house*: vaults for the storage
   of the bones of the dead.
73 *unmann'd*: Lady Macbeth challenges
   her husband's manhood; compare
   1, 7, 39–54.

75–6 *Blood . . . gentle weal*: there was
   bloodshed before now, in the olden
   days, before law and order ('humane
   statute') had regulated the nation.
78 *for the ear*: to speak about.

81 *twenty . . . crowns*: twenty fatal
   wounds in their heads; compare
   'twenty trenched gashes on his head'
   (line 27).

Macbeth

I do forget—

85 Do not muse at me, my most worthy friends.
I have a strange infirmity which is nothing
To those that know me. Come, love and health to all,
Then I'll sit down. Give me some wine; fill full!

Enter Ghost of Banquo

I drink to th'general joy o'th'whole table,
90 And to our dear friend Banquo, whom we miss.
Would he were here! To all, and him we thirst,
And all to all.

Lords

Our duties and the pledge.

Macbeth

Avaunt and quit my sight! Let the earth hide thee!
Thy bones are marrowless, thy blood is cold;
95 Thou hast no speculation in those eyes
Which thou dost glare with.

Lady Macbeth

Think of this, good peers,
But as a thing of custom. 'Tis no other,
Only it spoils the pleasure of the time.

Macbeth

What man dare, I dare;
100 Approach thou like the rugged Russian bear,
The arm'd rhinoceros, or th'Hyrcan tiger,
Take any shape but that, and my firm nerves
Shall never tremble. Or be alive again,
And dare me to the desert with thy sword;
105 If trembling I inhabit then, protest me
The baby of a girl. Hence horrible shadow,
Unreal mock'ry hence.   [*Exit* Ghost of Banquo

Why so, being gone,
I am a man again.—Pray you, sit still.

Lady Macbeth

You have displac'd the mirth, broke the good meeting
110 With most admir'd disorder.

---

87 *love . . . all*: Macbeth proposes a toast to ease the tension.

92 *pledge*: oath of allegiance.

95 *speculation*: power of seeing.

97 *a thing of custom*: a regular occurrence.

101 *arm'd*: i.e. with a thick skin and a tusk.
Hyrcan tiger: The tigers of Hyrcania (an area on the south-east coast of the Caspian Sea) were proverbially (and poetically) fierce.
102 *but that*: i.e. except that of Banquo's ghost.
104 *dare . . . desert*: challenge me to fight you in the wilderness.
105 *If trembling . . . then*: if I so much as tremble then.
protest: proclaim.
106 *baby*: doll, plaything.

110 *admir'd*: amazing, astonishing.

111 *overcome*: pass over.

112–13 *make . . . owe*: make me feel as though I'm not really myself.

113 *owe*: own.

115 *ruby*: redness.

116 *blanch'd*: turned white.

119 *Stand . . . going*: don't worry about the precedence of rank in your departure. Compare this disarray with the order of 'You know your own degrees' (line 1).

124–6 *Augures . . . blood*: speaking birds (such as magpies, jackdaws, and rooks) have given omens ('Augures') and signs have revealed the most hidden ('secret'st') murderer by means of talking birds.

124 *understood relations*: known relationships (e.g. between natural phenomena and events in the human world).

125 *maggot-pies*: magpies (which can imitate the human voice).
choughs: crows (birds of ill omen).

127 *at odds*: disputing with.

128 *denies his person*: refuses to come; Macduff's refusal is an insult, and an act of defiance.

131 *them*: the Scottish nobles.

132 *feed*: bribed—i.e. as a spy.

133 *betimes*: early, speedily.

134 *bent*: determined.

Macbeth
Can such things be,
And overcome us like a summer's cloud,
Without our special wonder? You make me strange
Even to the disposition that I owe,
When now I think you can behold such sights
115 And keep the natural ruby of your cheeks,
When mine is blanch'd with fear.
Ross
What sights, my lord?
Lady Macbeth
I pray you speak not; he grows worse and worse.
Question enrages him. At once, good night.
Stand not upon the order of your going,
120 But go at once.
Lennox
Good night, and better health
Attend his majesty.
Lady Macbeth
A kind good night to all.
[*Exeunt* Lords *and* Attendants
Macbeth
It will have blood they say: blood will have blood.
Stones have been known to move and trees to speak.
Augures, and understood relations, have
125 By maggot-pies, and choughs, and rooks brought forth
The secret'st man of blood. What is the night?
Lady Macbeth
Almost at odds with morning, which is which.
Macbeth
How sayst thou that Macduff denies his person
At our great bidding?
Lady Macbeth
Did you send to him, sir?
Macbeth
130 I hear it by the way, but I will send.
There's not a one of them but in his house
I keep a servant feed. I will tomorrow—
And betimes I will—to the weïrd sisters.
More shall they speak. For now I am bent to know
135 By the worst means, the worst; for mine own good,

All causes shall give way. I am in blood
Stepp'd in so far that should I wade no more,
Returning were as tedious as go o'er.
Strange things I have in head that will to hand,
140 Which must be acted ere they may be scann'd.
    Lady Macbeth
You lack the season of all natures, sleep.
    Macbeth
Come, we'll to sleep. My strange and self-abuse
Is the initiate fear that wants hard use;
We are yet but young in deed.   [*Exeunt*

138 *tedious*: troublesome.
    go o'er: crossing to the other side.
139 *will to hand*: need to be done.
140 *scann'd*: looked at closely.

141 *season*: preservative.
142 *My . . . self-abuse*: my uncharacteristic behaviour.
143 *the initiate fear*: a novice's fear.
    wants: lacks.
144 *young*: inexperienced.
    deed: action.

Act 3 Scene 5
The witches and their queen Hecate prepare for another meeting with Macbeth. This scene is not Shakespeare's work; see 'Source, Date, and Text', p.xxvii, and '*Macbeth*: the source', p.101.

Scene 5

A deserted place. Thunder. Enter the three Witches,
meeting Hecate

    First Witch
Why how now, Hecate, you look angerly?
    Hecate
Have I not reason, beldams, as you are,
Saucy and over-bold? How did you dare
To trade and traffic with Macbeth
5 In riddles and affairs of death?
And I the mistress of your charms,
The close contriver of all harms,
Was never call'd to bear my part
Or show the glory of our art?
10 And which is worse, all you have done
Hath been but for a wayward son,
Spiteful and wrathful, who, as others do,
Loves for his own ends, not for you.
But make amends now. Get you gone,
15 And at the pit of Acheron
Meet me i'th'morning. Thither he
Will come to know his destiny.
Your vessels and your spells provide,
Your charms and every thing beside.
20 I am for th'air. This night I'll spend

2 *beldams*: old hags.
3 *Saucy*: impudent.
4 *traffic*: deal.

7 *close contriver*: secret organizer.

9 *art*: witchcraft.

13 *Loves . . . you*: only cares about magic and prophecy for what they can do for him, and not for themselves.
15 *Acheron*: This was one of the rivers of Hades, the underworld of classical mythology.

Unto a dismal and a fatal end.
Great business must be wrought ere noon.
Upon the corner of the moon
There hangs a vap'rous drop profound;
25 I'll catch it ere it come to ground;
And that distill'd by magic sleights,
Shall raise such artificial sprites
As by the strength of their illusion
Shall draw him on to his confusion.
30 He shall spurn fate, scorn death, and bear
His hopes 'bove wisdom, grace, and fear.
And you all know, security
Is mortals' chiefest enemy.

Music, and a song, 'Come away, come away', within

Hark, I am call'd: my little spirit, see,
35 Sits in a foggy cloud, and stays for me.   [*Exit*
First Witch
Come, let's make haste; she'll soon be back again.
[*Exeunt*

24 *vap'rous drop*: It was believed that
witches could invoke the moon to
shed a malign influence on herbs and
other objects.
profound: deep, with hidden qualities.
26 *sleights*: tricks, artifice.
27 *artificial sprites*: wicked spirits made
by art (i.e. not the real demonic
powers).
29 *confusion*: ruin, damnation.

32–3 *security . . . enemy*: Proverbial: 'the
way to be safe is never to be secure'.
32 *security*: over-confidence,
complacency.
33s.d. *Music . . . song*: The song may
have been that in the play *The Witch*
by Thomas Middleton (see '*Macbeth*:
the source', p.101).

Scene 6

Somewhere in Scotland: enter Lennox *and another*
Lord

Lennox
My former speeches have but hit your thoughts
Which can interpret further; only I say
Things have been strangely borne. The gracious
Duncan
Was pitied of Macbeth; marry, he was dead.
5 And the right-valiant Banquo walk'd too late,
Whom you may say, if't please you, Fleance kill'd,
For Fleance fled. Men must not walk too late.
Who cannot want the thought how monstrous
It was for Malcolm and for Donaldbain
10 To kill their gracious father? Damned fact,
How it did grieve Macbeth! Did he not straight

Act 3 Scene 6
Lennox and an unnamed Lord discuss the
state of affairs: Malcolm is in England;
Macduff has gone to join him; and the
English king is raising an army to fight
against Macbeth.

1 *hit*: touched.

3 *borne*: managed, carried out.

4 *pitied of*: lamented by. Lennox is
choosing his words very carefully.
Marry: by [the Virgin] Mary; a mild
oath, meaning no more than 'yes,
indeed'.

8 *cannot . . . thought*: can fail to think.

10 *Damned*: damnèd.
fact: deed.
11 *straight*: immediately.

12 *pious*: dutiful, loyal.
13 *thralls*: captives.

16 *deny't*: deny that they had murdered Duncan.
17 *He*: i.e. Macbeth.
18 *under his key*: locked up in his power.
19 *an't please*: if it please.

21 *broad words*: unguarded gossip.
21–2 *he . . . feast*: failed to attend Macbeth's banquet; see *3, 4, 128*.

24 *bestows himself*: has hidden himself.
son of Duncan: Malcolm.

25 *holds*: withholds.
the due of birth: his birthright—i.e. the crown.
27 *Of*: by.
Edward: Edward the Confessor, King of England 1042–66.
28–9 *That . . . respect*: Malcolm's present misfortunes have not affected him in Edward's high esteem.
30 *upon his aid*: in support of Malcolm.
31 *Northumberland . . . Siward*: Siward, Earl of Northumberland, and Young Siward, his son.
32 *him above*: God.
33 *ratify*: make valid, sanction.
36 *faithful*: sincere.
free honours: honest rewards.

38 *exasperate*: exasperated, infuriated.

40 *he*: i.e. Macbeth.

41 *'Sir, not I'*: This was Macduff's reply to Macbeth.
42 *cloudy*: frowning.
turns me his back: goes and turns his back; 'me' is used in this phrase merely for emphasis.
43 *hums*: murmurs.
44 *clogs*: burdens; the Messenger probably knows Macbeth's treatment of those who bring bad news.

In pious rage the two delinquents tear,
That were the slaves of drink and thralls of sleep?
Was not that nobly done? Ay, and wisely too,
15 For 'twould have anger'd any heart alive
To hear the men deny't. So that I say,
He has borne all things well, and I do think
That had he Duncan's sons under his key—
As, an't please heaven, he shall not—they should find
20 What 'twere to kill a father. So should Fleance.
But peace, for from broad words, and 'cause he fail'd
His presence at the tyrant's feast, I hear
Macduff lives in disgrace. Sir, can you tell
Where he bestows himself?

Lord

                                    The son of Duncan,
25 From whom this tyrant holds the due of birth,
Lives in the English court and is receiv'd
Of the most pious Edward with such grace,
That the malevolence of fortune nothing
Takes from his high respect. Thither Macduff
30 Is gone to pray the holy king upon his aid
To wake Northumberland and warlike Siward,
That by the help of these, with him above
To ratify the work, we may again
Give to our tables meat, sleep to our nights,
35 Free from our feasts and banquets bloody knives,
Do faithful homage and receive free honours,
All which we pine for now. And this report
Hath so exasperate their king that he
Prepares for some attempt of war.

Lennox

40 Sent he to Macduff?

Lord

He did. And with an absolute, 'Sir, not I',
The cloudy messenger turns me his back
And hums, as who should say, 'You'll rue the time
That clogs me with this answer.'

Lennox

And that well might
45 Advise him to a caution t'hold what distance
His wisdom can provide. Some holy angel
Fly to the court of England and unfold
His message ere he come, that a swift blessing
May soon return to this our suffering country
50 Under a hand accurs'd.

Lord

I'll send my prayers with him.
[*Exeunt*

45–6 *Advise . . . provide*: warn him to stay as far away (from Macbeth) as he knows how.

ACT 4

Act 4 **Scene 1**

The witches assemble to meet Macbeth, and promise to answer his questions. Their magic Apparitions comfort him at first—and then give cause for alarm.

1 *brindled cat*: cat with black/brown streaked fur.

2 *hedge-pig*: hedgehog.

3 *Harpier*: This is presumably the name of the witch's 'familiar', or attendant spirit.

8 *Swelter'd . . . got*: sweated out poison incubated in sleep; the ingredients of the witches' cooking-pot are all items thought by the Elizabethans to be poisonous or unnatural.
9 *charmed*: charmèd.

12 *Fillet . . . snake*: lengthwise slice of a snake from the fens.

15 *Wool of bat*: short hair from the skin of a bat.
16 *fork*: forked tongue.
blind-worm: slow-worm (a kind of legless lizard).
17 *howlet*: young owl.
19 *hell-broth*: thick soup, strong enough for the devil.

23 *mummy*: mummia, a preparation used in embalming bodies, or taken from embalmed bodies.
maw and gulf: stomach and throat.

SCENE 1

An isolated place. Thunder. Enter the three Witches with a cauldron

First Witch
Thrice the brindled cat hath mew'd.
   Second Witch
Thrice and once the hedge-pig whin'd.
   Third Witch
Harpier cries, ' 'Tis time, 'tis time.'
   First Witch
Round about the cauldron go;
5 In the poison'd entrails throw.
Toad, that under cold stone
Days and nights has thirty-one
Swelter'd venom sleeping got,
Boil thou first i'th'charmed pot.
   All
10 Double, double toil and trouble;
Fire burn, and cauldron bubble.
   Second Witch
Fillet of a fenny snake,
In the cauldron boil and bake:
Eye of newt, and toe of frog,
15 Wool of bat, and tongue of dog,
Adder's fork, and blind-worm's sting,
Lizard's leg, and howlet's wing,
For a charm of powerful trouble,
Like a hell-broth, boil and bubble.
   All
20 Double, double toil and trouble,
Fire burn, and cauldron bubble.
   Third Witch
Scale of dragon, tooth of wolf,
Witches' mummy, maw and gulf

'I conjure you by that which you profess', (4, 1, 49). Lennie James as Macbeth, Tricycle Theatre, London, 1995.

24 *ravin'd*: ravenous.
25 *hemlock*: i.e. the 'insane root'
   (compare *1, 3, 82*).
   digg'd . . . dark: Night-time was best
   for gathering poisonous herbs and
   roots.
27 *slips*: cuttings.
26–9 *blaspheming . . . lips*: The bodily
   parts are all those of infidels.
27 *goat*: Traditionally a lecherous beast.
31 *Ditch-deliver'd*: born in a ditch.
   drab: prostitute.
32 *slab*: semi-solid.
33 *chawdron*: entrails.
34 *ingredience*: mixture of ingredients.

37 *baboon*: Another traditionally evil and
   lustful creature.

38s.d.–43s.d. *Enter Hecate . . . Witches*:
   These lines (like the whole of *Act 3,
   Scene 5*) are almost certainly not
   Shakespeare's work; see 'Source,
   Date, and Text', p.xxvii, and '*Macbeth*:
   the source', p.101.
39 *I . . . pains*: I appreciate the trouble
   you have taken.

Of the ravin'd salt-sea shark,
25 Root of hemlock, digg'd i'th'dark;
Liver of blaspheming Jew,
Gall of goat, and slips of yew,
Sliver'd in the moon's eclipse;
Nose of Turk, and Tartar's lips,
30 Finger of birth-strangl'd babe,
Ditch-deliver'd by a drab,
Make the gruel thick and slab.
Add thereto a tiger's chawdron
For th'ingredience of our cauldron.
   All
35 Double, double toil and trouble,
Fire burn, and cauldron bubble.
   Second Witch
Cool it with a baboon's blood,
Then the charm is firm and good.

Enter Hecate, *and the other three* Witches

   Hecate
O well done! I commend your pains,
40 And every one shall share i'th'gains;
And now about the cauldron sing
Like elves and fairies in a ring,
Enchanting all that you put in.

Music, and a song, 'Black spirits, etc.'
   [*Exeunt* Hecate *and the other three* Witches
   Second Witch
By the pricking of my thumbs,
45 Something wicked this way comes;
Open locks, whoever knocks.

Enter Macbeth

   Macbeth
How now, you secret, black, and midnight hags!
What is't you do?
   All the Witches

                              A deed without a name.

49 *conjure . . . profess*: call upon you
   solemnly in the name of that magic
   you practise ('profess').
51–9 *Though . . . sicken*: Macbeth is
   prepared to risk all the common
   hazards of witchcraft.
52 *yeasty*: frothy, foaming (like a liquid
   when yeast has been added).
53 *navigation*: shipping.
54 *bladed corn*: unripe corn (where the
   'blade' still surrounds the 'ear').
   lodg'd: flattened, broken down (by
   wind and rain).
56 *pyramids*: obelisks, pillars.
58 *nature's germen*: seeds, basic matter,
   of all creation; compare 'seeds of
   time' (*1, 3, 56*).
59 *till destruction sicken*: until
   destruction itself is sick (because so
   much has been destroyed).

62 *our masters'*: the mouths of our
   masters—i.e. the evil spirits that the
   witches serve.
64 *nine farrow*: litter of nine piglets.
   sweaten: exuded.

65 *gibbet*: gallows.

67 *office*: function.
67s.d. *armed*: armoured, helmeted.

Macbeth
I conjure you by that which you profess,
50 Howe'er you come to know it, answer me.
Though you untie the winds and let them fight
Against the churches, though the yeasty waves
Confound and swallow navigation up,
Though bladed corn be lodg'd and trees blown down,
55 Though castles topple on their warders' heads,
Though palaces and pyramids do slope
Their heads to their foundations, though the treasure
Of nature's germen tumble altogether
Even till destruction sicken: answer me
60 To what I ask you.
First Witch
                        Speak.
Second Witch
                              Demand.
Third Witch
                                    We'll answer.
First Witch
Say, if thou'dst rather hear it from our mouths,
Or from our masters'?
Macbeth
                        Call 'em, let me see 'em.
First Witch
Pour in sow's blood, that hath eaten
Her nine farrow; grease that's sweaten
65 From the murderer's gibbet throw
Into the flame.
All the Witches
                              Come high or low:
Thyself and office deftly show.

Thunder. Enter First Apparition, *an armed Head*

Macbeth
Tell me, thou unknown power—
First Witch
                                    He knows thy thought:
Hear his speech, but say thou nought.

First Apparition

70 Macbeth, Macbeth, Macbeth: beware Macduff,
Beware the Thane of Fife. Dismiss me. Enough.

[*Descends*

Macbeth

Whate'er thou art, for thy good caution, thanks;
Thou hast harp'd my fear aright. But one word more—

First Witch

He will not be commanded. Here's another,

75 More potent than the first.

Thunder. Enter Second Apparition, *a bloody Child*

Second Apparition

Macbeth, Macbeth, Macbeth.

Macbeth

Had I three ears, I'd hear thee.

Second Apparition

Be bloody, bold, and resolute; laugh to scorn
The power of man, for none of woman born

80 Shall harm Macbeth.

[*Descends*

Macbeth

Then live, Macduff, what need I fear of thee?
But yet I'll make assurance double sure
And take a bond of fate: thou shalt not live,
That I may tell pale-hearted fear it lies,

85 And sleep in spite of thunder.

Thunder. Enter Third Apparition, *a Child crowned
with a tree in his hand*

What is this,
That rises like the issue of a king
And wears upon his baby-brow the round
And top of sovereignty?

All the Witches

Listen, but speak not to't.

Third Apparition

Be lion-mettl'd, proud, and take no care

90 Who chafes, who frets, or where conspirers are.
Macbeth shall never vanquish'd be until

71 *Thane of Fife*: Macduff; see '*Macbeth: the source*', p.101.
71s.d. *Descends*: This stage direction from the Folio text suggests that the Apparitions would disappear through a trap-door in the stage.
72 *caution*: warning.
73 *harp'd*: guessed, hit upon.

83 *bond*: contract, legal surety; by killing Macduff, Macbeth will guarantee that Fate will keep the promise of the second Apparition.
84 *That . . . lies*: so that I can tell these cowardly fears they are false.
86 *issue*: descendant.

87–8 *round . . . sovereignty*: the crown.
88 *speak not to't*: Spectators were usually warned to keep silent in the presence of supernatural phenomena.
89 *lion-mettl'd*: lion-hearted.
90 *chafes*: is angry.
   frets: complains.

Great Birnam Wood to high Dunsinane Hill
Shall come against him.   [*Descends*
   Macbeth
                         That will never be:
Who can impress the forest, bid the tree
95 Unfix his earthbound root? Sweet bodements, good.
Rebellious dead, rise never till the wood
Of Birnam rise, and our high-plac'd Macbeth
Shall live the lease of nature, pay his breath
To time and mortal custom. Yet my heart
100 Throbs to know one thing. Tell me, if your art
Can tell so much, shall Banquo's issue ever
Reign in this kingdom?
   All the Witches
                         Seek to know no more.
   Macbeth
I will be satisfied. Deny me this,
And an eternal curse fall on you. Let me know.

Cauldron descends. Hautboys

105 Why sinks that cauldron? And what noise is this?
   First Witch
Show!
   Second Witch
Show!
   Third Witch
Show!
   All the Witches
Show his eyes and grieve his heart,
110 Come like shadows, so depart.

*Enter a show of eight kings, and the last with a glass
in his hand; Banquo's Ghost following*

   Macbeth
Thou art too like the spirit of Banquo. Down!
Thy crown does sear mine eyeballs. And thy hair,
Thou other gold-bound brow, is like the first;
A third, is like the former.—Filthy hags,

115 *Start, eyes*: let my eyes jump out of
   my head.
116 *crack of doom*: break of Judgement
   Day (Doomsday).

120 *two-fold . . . sceptres*: i.e. the twin
   orbs of the English and Scottish
   crowns, and the sceptres of England,
   Scotland, and Wales.
122 *blood-bolter'd*: covered in clotted
   blood.

125 *amazedly*: bewildered.

129 *antic round*: grotesque dance (perhaps
   in a circle round Macbeth).

131 *Our . . . pay*: our homage has given
   him the welcome he deserves.

133 *aye*: for ever.
   accursed: accursèd.
134 *without there*: whoever is outside
   (offstage).

115 Why do you show me this?—A fourth? Start, eyes!
What, will the line stretch out to th'crack of doom?
Another yet? A seventh? I'll see no more.
And yet the eighth appears, who bears a glass
Which shows me many more. And some I see,
120 That two-fold balls and treble sceptres carry.
Horrible sight! Now I see 'tis true,
For the blood-bolter'd Banquo smiles upon me,
And points at them for his.
                    [*Exeunt show of kings and* Banquo's Ghost
                              What, is this so?

First Witch
Ay, sir, all this is so. But why
125 Stands Macbeth thus amazedly?
Come, sisters, cheer we up his sprites,
And show the best of our delights.
I'll charm the air to give a sound,
While you perform your antic round
130 That this great king may kindly say,
Our duties did his welcome pay.

Music. The Witches *dance, and vanish*

Macbeth
Where are they? Gone? Let this pernicious hour,
Stand aye accursed in the calendar.
Come in, without there!

Enter Lennox

Lennox
                         What's your grace's will?
Macbeth
135 Saw you the weïrd sisters?
Lennox
                              No, my lord.
Macbeth
Came they not by you?
Lennox
                         No indeed, my lord.

Macbeth
Infected be the air whereon they ride,
And damn'd all those that trust them. I did hear
The galloping of horse. Who was't came by?
Lennox
140 'Tis two or three, my lord, that bring you word
Macduff is fled to England.
Macbeth
Fled to England?
Lennox
Ay, my good lord.
Macbeth
[*Aside*] Time, thou anticipat'st my dread exploits;
The flighty purpose never is o'ertook
145 Unless the deed go with it. From this moment,
The very firstlings of my heart shall be
The firstlings of my hand. And even now
To crown my thoughts with acts, be it thought and
done.
The castle of Macduff I will surprise;
150 Seize upon Fife; give to th'edge o'th'sword
His wife, his babes, and all unfortunate souls
That trace him in his line. No boasting like a fool;
This deed I'll do before this purpose cool,
But no more sights.—Where are these gentlemen?
155 Come, bring me where they are.   [*Exeunt*

SCENE 2

Fife: Macduff's castle. Enter Lady Macduff, *her* son,
and Ross

Lady Macduff
What had he done, to make him fly the land?
Ross
You must have patience, madam.
Lady Macduff
He had none;
His flight was madness. When our actions do not,
Our fears do make us traitors.

143 *dread*: terrible.
144–5 *The . . . with it*: it's impossible to act as quick as thought unless intention and action go together.
146–7 *The firstlings . . . hand*: as soon as I get an idea, I'll carry it out. *firstlings*: firstborn things.

152 *trace . . . line*: descend from him, are of his lineage.

Act 4 Scene 2
Lady Macduff questions Ross about her husband's flight, and then tries to explain the situation to her son. A Messenger warns her to make a quick getaway, but Macbeth's murderers burst into the room before she can take his advice.

3–4 *When . . . traitors*: even when we have done nothing, we are still traitors for running away in fear.

Ross

                                  You know not
5 Whether it was his wisdom or his fear.
      Lady Macduff
  Wisdom? To leave his wife, to leave his babes,
  His mansion, and his titles in a place
  From whence himself does fly? He loves us not.
  He wants the natural touch, for the poor wren,
10 The most diminutive of birds, will fight,
  Her young ones in her nest, against the owl.
  All is the fear, and nothing is the love;
  As little is the wisdom, where the flight
  So runs against all reason.
      Ross
                          My dearest coz,
15 I pray you school yourself. But for your husband,
  He is noble, wise, judicious, and best knows
  The fits o'th'season. I dare not speak much further,
  But cruel are the times when we are traitors
  And do not know ourselves, when we hold rumour
20 From what we fear, yet know not what we fear,
  But float upon a wild and violent sea,
  Each way and none. I take my leave of you;
  Shall not be long but I'll be here again.
  Things at the worst will cease, or else climb upward
25 To what they were before. My pretty cousin,
  Blessing upon you.
      Lady Macduff
  Father'd he is, and yet he's fatherless.
      Ross
  I am so much a fool, should I stay longer
  It would be my disgrace and your discomfort.
30 I take my leave at once.   *[Exit*
      Lady Macduff
                     Sirrah, your father's dead,
  And what will you do now? How will you live?
      Son
  As birds do, mother.
      Lady Macduff
                   What, with worms and flies?

---

7 *titles*: entitlements, the things belonging to his title of nobility.

9 *wants . . . touch*: lacks natural feelings.

12–14 *All . . . reason*: when it is so unreasonable to run away, it shows neither concern for his family ('love') nor wisdom, but only selfish fear.

14 *coz*: cousin (a general term of endearment).
15 *school*: control.
    for: as for.
17 *fits o'th'season*: mood of the times.
18–19 *when . . . ourselves*: we behave in uncharacteristic ways and don't know what we are doing.
19–20 *hold . . . fear*: believe rumours because we are fearful.
22 *Each . . . none*: this way and that, and get nowhere in the end.
23 *Shall . . . again*: it won't be long before I come back.
24 *climb upward*: get better, improve.

29 *It would . . . discomfort*: Ross is afraid that he will be moved to tears, embarrassing himself and Lady Macduff.
30 *Sirrah*: A term of endearment (as used here), abuse, or condescension.

34–5 *net . . . gin*: Lady Macduff lists
         different methods of catching birds.
34 *lime*: sticky lime on tree branches.
35 *pitfall*: covered hole.
         gin: snare.
36 *Poor . . . for*: traps aren't set for fowls
         of inferior species.

Son
With what I get I mean, and so do they.
   Lady Macduff
Poor bird, thou'dst never fear the net, nor lime, the
35 pitfall, nor the gin.
   Son
Why should I, mother? Poor birds they are not set for.
My father is not dead for all your saying.
   Lady Macduff
Yes, he is dead. How wilt thou do for a father?
   Son
Nay, how will you do for a husband?
   Lady Macduff
40 Why, I can buy me twenty at any market.
   Son
Then you'll buy 'em to sell again.
   Lady Macduff
Thou speak'st with all thy wit, and yet i'faith with wit
enough for thee.

41 *Then . . . again*: if you can get them
         so easily, you will not want to keep
         them.
42 *wit*: intelligence.
43 *for thee*: for your age.

   Son
Was my father a traitor, mother?
   Lady Macduff
45 Ay, that he was.
   Son
What is a traitor?
   Lady Macduff
Why, one that swears and lies.

47 *swears*: takes an oath.

   Son
And be all traitors, that do so?
   Lady Macduff
Every one that does so is a traitor and must be hanged.
   Son
50 And must they all be hanged that swear and lie?
   Lady Macduff
Every one.
   Son
Who must hang them?
   Lady Macduff
Why, the honest men.

Son

Then the liars and swearers are fools, for there are liars
55 and swearers enough to beat the honest men and hang
them up.

Lady Macduff

Now God help thee, poor monkey, but how wilt thou do
for a father?

Son

If he were dead, you'd weep for him; if you would not, it
60 were a good sign that I should quickly have a new father.

Lady Macduff

Poor prattler, how thou talk'st!

Enter a Messenger

Messenger

Bless you, fair dame. I am not to you known,
Though in your state of honour I am perfect;
I doubt some danger does approach you nearly.
65 If you will take a homely man's advice,
Be not found here. Hence with your little ones.
To fright you thus, methinks I am too savage;
To do worse to you were fell cruelty,
Which is too nigh your person. Heaven preserve you,
70 I dare abide no longer.   [*Exit*

Lady Macduff

                Whither should I fly?
I have done no harm. But I remember now
I am in this earthly world where to do harm
Is often laudable, to do good sometime
Accounted dangerous folly. Why then, alas,
75 Do I put up that womanly defence,
To say I have done no harm?

Enter Murderers

                     What are these faces?

A Murderer

Where is your husband?

---

63 *in your state . . . perfect*: I know your rank and reputation very well.
64 *doubt*: fear, suspect.
65 *homely*: humble.

68 *fell*: pitiless.
69 *nigh*: near.

78 *unsanctified*: accursed.

Lady Macduff
I hope in no place so unsanctified,
Where such as thou mayst find him.
A Murderer
                                        He's a traitor.
Son
80 Thou liest, thou shag-hair'd villain.
A Murderer
                                        What, you egg!

80 *egg*: youngster.
81 *fry*: spawn, offspring.

Young fry of treachery!

Kills him

Son
                              He has kill'd me, mother.
Run away, I pray you!
                    [*Exit* Lady Macduff *crying 'Murder', pursued by*
                              Murderers *with her* Son

Act 4 Scene 3
At the English court Malcolm and Macduff
test each other's loyalties. There are plans
to attack Macbeth—and Macduff hears the
news of the murder of his wife and
children.

SCENE 3

The English Court: enter Malcolm *and* Macduff

Malcolm
Let us seek out some desolate shade and there
Weep our sad bosoms empty.
Macduff
                              Let us rather
Hold fast the mortal sword and like good men
Bestride our downfall birthdom; each new morn,
3 *mortal*: deadly, death-dealing.
3–4 *like . . . birthdom*: protect the
country of our birth from ruin as good
soldiers stand astride a fallen
comrade.

5 New widows howl, new orphans cry, new sorrows
Strike heaven on the face, that it resounds
As if it felt with Scotland and yell'd out
Like syllable of dolour.

8 *Like*: the same.
wail: lament, grieve for.

Malcolm
                                        What I believe, I'll wail;
What know, believe; and what I can redress,

9 *What . . . believe*: only believe what I
know to be true.
redress: put right.
10 *As . . . friend*: when the time is right.
11 *What . . . perchance*: perhaps what
you say is true.
12 *sole name*: name alone.

10 As I shall find the time to friend, I will.
What you have spoke, it may be so perchance.
This tyrant, whose sole name blisters our tongues,
Was once thought honest; you have lov'd him well—

14 *touch'd*: harmed.
14–15 *something . . . me*: you may gain something from him through betraying me.
wisdom: it is wisdom.
16 *innocent lamb*: The image of the sacrificial lamb is central to the Christian religion.

19–20 *A good . . . charge*: Malcolm suggests that Macduff's honourable nature may have degenerated under Macbeth's government.
21 *That . . . transpose*: my suspicious thoughts can't change your nature.
22 *Angels . . . fell*: there are still some bright-shining angels, although the brightest of them fell from God's grace.
the brightest: Lucifer ('the light-bearer') who rebelled against God and was thrown down from heaven (Isaiah 14: 4,12).
23–4 *Though . . . so*: if everything that's evil tried to look virtuous, virtue would still look the same.
23 *brows*: forehead, appearance.
25 *Perchance*: perhaps.
even there: i.e. in Macduff's flight to England: Macduff had been hoping that he could overthrow Macbeth—but his sudden flight to England has aroused Malcolm's suspicions.
26 *rawness*: exposed situation.
27 *motives*: reasons for staying in Scotland.
knots: ties.
29–30 *Let . . . safeties*: my suspicions are not meant to dishonour you but to protect myself.
32–3 *tyranny . . . check thee*: tyranny can make itself secure, since virtue—Malcolm—dare not oppose it.
33–4 *wear . . . affeer'd*: Macbeth can wear his stolen crown because his title to it is legally confirmed ('affeer'd' is a legal term) by Malcolm's ineffectiveness.
37 *to boot*: in addition.
38 *in absolute fear*: entirely in fear.
39 *the yoke*: i.e. Macbeth's government; the 'yoke' fastens oxen to the plough.
41 *withal*: as well.

He hath not touch'd you yet. I am young, but something
15 You may discern of him through me, and wisdom
To offer up a weak, poor innocent lamb
T'appease an angry god.
Macduff
I am not treacherous.
Malcolm
But Macbeth is.
A good and virtuous nature may recoil
20 In an imperial charge. But I shall crave your pardon:
That which you are, my thoughts cannot transpose;
Angels are bright still, though the brightest fell.
Though all things foul would wear the brows of grace,
Yet grace must still look so.
Macduff
I have lost my hopes.
Malcolm
25 Perchance even there where I did find my doubts.
Why in that rawness left you wife and child,
Those precious motives, those strong knots of love,
Without leave-taking? I pray you,
Let not my jealousies be your dishonours,
30 But mine own safeties; you may be rightly just,
Whatever I shall think.
Macduff
Bleed, bleed, poor country.
Great tyranny, lay thou thy basis sure,
For goodness dare not check thee; wear thou thy wrongs,
The title is affeer'd. Fare thee well, lord,
35 I would not be the villain that thou think'st
For the whole space that's in the tyrant's grasp,
And the rich East to boot.
Malcolm
Be not offended.
I speak not as in absolute fear of you:
I think our country sinks beneath the yoke;
40 It weeps, it bleeds, and each new day a gash
Is added to her wounds. I think withal
There would be hands uplifted in my right,

43 *England*: the King of England, Edward the Confessor.

48–9 *More . . . succeed*: suffer more, and in many more different ways, under his successor; see '*Macbeth*: the source', p.101.

51 *grafted*: made part of me (as gardeners graft plants together).
52 *open'd*: i.e. like buds; Malcolm continues the gardening image.

55 *confineless harms*: boundless injuries. *legions*: multitudes, battalions.

58 *Luxurious*: lascivious, lecherous.
59 *Sudden*: rash, impulsive. *smacking*: tasting.

63 *cistern*: tank, container of fluids.
63–5 *my desire . . . will*: my lust would overflow all barriers of restraint that opposed me.

66–7 *Boundless . . . tyranny*: lack of self-control is a tyranny in a man's character.
67–8 *it hath . . . throne*: it has caused many thrones to become vacant prematurely.

71 *Convey . . . plenty*: have plenty of scope to carry on as you please.
72 *hoodwink*: deceive (by blindfolding).

74 *vulture*: The bird is the epitome of greediness.

And here from gracious England have I offer
Of goodly thousands. But for all this,
45 When I shall tread upon the tyrant's head,
Or wear it on my sword, yet my poor country
Shall have more vices than it had before,
More suffer, and more sundry ways than ever,
By him that shall succeed.

Macduff
                              What should he be?

Malcolm
50 It is myself I mean—in whom I know
All the particulars of vice so grafted
Than when they shall be open'd, black Macbeth
Will seem as pure as snow, and the poor state
Esteem him as a lamb, being compar'd
55 With my confineless harms.

Macduff
                          Not in the legions
Of horrid hell can come a devil more damn'd
In evils to top Macbeth.

Malcolm
                          I grant him bloody,
Luxurious, avaricious, false, deceitful,
Sudden, malicious, smacking of every sin
60 That has a name. But there's no bottom, none,
In my voluptuousness: your wives, your daughters,
Your matrons, and your maids could not fill up
The cistern of my lust, and my desire
All continent impediments would o'erbear
65 That did oppose my will. Better Macbeth,
Than such an one to reign.

Macduff
                          Boundless intemperance
In nature is a tyranny; it hath been
Th'untimely emptying of the happy throne
And fall of many kings. But fear not yet
70 To take upon you what is yours: you may
Convey your pleasures in a spacious plenty
And yet seem cold. The time you may so hoodwink.
We have willing dames enough; there cannot be
That vulture in you to devour so many

75–6 *dedicate . . . inclin'd*: offer
themselves in (sexual) service to the
king as soon as they know he likes
that sort of thing.

77 *ill-compos'd affection*: unbalanced
disposition.
78 *stanchless*: unstoppable, insatiable.
79 *cut off*: put to death.
80 *his . . . house*: this man's jewels, and
that man's house.
81–2 *my . . . more*: the more I had, the
more I would want.

85 *Sticks deeper*: is more deeply rooted.

86 *summer-seeming lust*: lust which is
hot but transitory, lasting only for the
summer of a man's life.
87 *sword . . . kings*: the death of some
Scottish kings.
88–9 *Scotland . . . own*: you have rich
harvests ('foisons') of your own in
Scotland that should satisfy you.
89 *portable*: bearable.
90 *weigh'd*: balanced.
91 *king-becoming graces*: virtues
appropriate for a king.
93 *perseverance*: The stress is on the
second syllable.
95 *relish*: trace.
96 *division*: variation.
several: particular, individual.
97–8 *I should . . . hell*: I would say 'To
hell with all harmony'.
99 *Uproar*: cause uproar among.

104 *untitl'd*: illegitimate, having no right
to the title.
bloody-sceptr'd: holding the sceptre
through bloodshed.

75 As will to greatness dedicate themselves,
Finding it so inclin'd.
  Malcolm
                                    With this, there grows
In my most ill-compos'd affection such
A stanchless avarice that, were I king,
I should cut off the nobles for their lands,
80 Desire his jewels, and this other's house,
And my more-having would be as a sauce
To make me hunger more, that I should forge
Quarrels unjust against the good and loyal,
Destroying them for wealth.
  Macduff
                                    This avarice
85 Sticks deeper, grows with more pernicious root
Than summer-seeming lust, and it hath been
The sword of our slain kings; yet do not fear,
Scotland hath foisons to fill up your will
Of your mere own. All these are portable,
90 With other graces weigh'd.
  Malcolm
But I have none. The king-becoming graces—
As justice, verity, temp'rance, stableness,
Bounty, perseverance, mercy, lowliness,
Devotion, patience, courage, fortitude—
95 I have no relish of them, but abound
In the division of each several crime,
Acting it many ways. Nay, had I power, I should
Pour the sweet milk of concord into hell,
Uproar the universal peace, confound
100 All unity on earth.
  Macduff
                                    O Scotland, Scotland!
  Malcolm
If such a one be fit to govern, speak.
I am as I have spoken.
  Macduff
                                    Fit to govern?
No, not to live. O nation miserable!
With an untitl'd tyrant, bloody-sceptr'd,

107–8 *By . . . breed*: by his own act convicts himself of treachery, and defames his own birth and heritage.

107 *interdiction*: legal restraint placed on those incapable of managing their own affairs.

111 *Died . . . lived*: lived each day as though it were her last; compare St Paul's claim, 'I die daily' (1 Corinthians 15:31).

112–13 *These . . . Scotland*: it's just those crimes you accuse yourself of [committed by Macbeth] that have forced me to leave Scotland.

115 *Child of integrity*: Macduff's grief for Scotland could only spring from his honesty.

116 *scruples*: doubts.

118 *trains*: stratagems.

119–20 *modest . . . haste*: cautious wisdom prevents me from trusting people too quickly.

123–4 *abjure . . . myself*: renounce all the accusations I made against myself.

126 *Unknown to woman*: a virgin. *was forsworn*: committed perjury.

133 *here-approach*: coming here.

134 *Old Siward*: The Earl of Northumberland.

135 *at a point*: in readiness.

136 *we'll together*: we'll go together.

136–7 *chance . . . quarrel*: may our chances of success be as good as our cause is lawful.

139 *'Tis . . . reconcile*: Macduff is not completely convinced by Malcolm. *more anon*: we'll talk more about it later.

105   When shalt thou see thy wholesome days again,
Since that the truest issue of thy throne
By his own interdiction stands accurs'd
And does blaspheme his breed? Thy royal father
Was a most sainted king; the queen that bore thee,
110   Oft'ner upon her knees than on her feet,
Died every day she lived. Fare thee well,
These evils thou repeat'st upon thyself
Hath banish'd me from Scotland. O my breast,
Thy hope ends here.
       Malcolm
                    Macduff, this noble passion,
115   Child of integrity, hath from my soul
Wip'd the black scruples, reconcil'd my thoughts
To thy good truth and honour. Devilish Macbeth
By many of these trains hath sought to win me
Into his power, and modest wisdom plucks me
120   From over-credulous haste; but God above
Deal between thee and me, for even now
I put myself to thy direction and
Unspeak mine own detraction, here abjure
The taints and blames I laid upon myself,
125   For strangers to my nature. I am yet
Unknown to woman, never was forsworn,
Scarcely have coveted what was mine own,
At no time broke my faith, would not betray
The devil to his fellow, and delight
130   No less in truth than life. My first false speaking
Was this upon myself. What I am truly
Is thine, and my poor country's, to command:
Whither indeed, before thy here-approach,
Old Siward with ten thousand warlike men
135   Already at a point was setting forth.
Now we'll together, and the chance of goodness
Be like our warranted quarrel. Why are you silent?
       Macduff
Such welcome and unwelcome things at once,
'Tis hard to reconcile.

Enter a Doctor

Malcolm
                                        Well, more anon.—
140 Comes the king forth, I pray you?
        Doctor
Ay, sir: there are a crew of wretched souls
That stay his cure; their malady convinces
The great assay of art, but at his touch,
Such sanctity hath heaven given his hand,
145 They presently amend.   [*Exit*
        Malcolm
I thank you, doctor.
        Macduff
What's the disease he means?
        Malcolm
'Tis called the Evil.
A most miraculous work in this good king,
150 Which often since my here-remain in England
I have seen him do. How he solicits heaven
Himself best knows, but strangely visited people
All swoll'n and ulcerous, pitiful to the eye,
The mere despair of surgery, he cures,
155 Hanging a golden stamp about their necks
Put on with holy prayers, and 'tis spoken
To the succeeding royalty he leaves
The healing benediction. With this strange virtue,
He hath a heavenly gift of prophecy,
160 And sundry blessings hang about his throne
That speak him full of grace.

        Enter Ross

        Macduff
                                        See who comes here.
        Malcolm
My countryman, but yet I know him not.
        Macduff
My ever gentle cousin, welcome hither.

142 *stay his cure*: wait for his healing touch; Edward the Confessor was thought to possess a heavenly power, which he bequeathed to succeeding monarchs, to cure scrofula—an inflammation of the lymph nodes which was popularly known as the 'King's Evil'.
convinces: overcomes, baffles.
143 *great . . . art*: greatest efforts of medical skill.
145 *presently amend*: recover at once.

151 *solicits*: entreats.
152 *visited*: afflicted.

154 *mere*: complete.
155 *stamp*: coin, medal; Queen Elizabeth and King James both gave coins to those they 'touched'.

158 *healing benediction*: blessed gift of healing.
162 *My . . . not*: Ross is probably identifiable as a Scot by his tartan clothing.
163 *ever gentle*: always noble.

164 *betimes*: as soon as possible.
165 *means*: circumstances.

166 *Stands . . . did*: is Scotland still the same as it was.

168–9 *nothing . . . smile*: the only people to smile are those who don't know what's going on.
169 *once*: ever.

172 *modern ecstasy*: everyday emotion.
172–3 *The deadman's . . . who*: hardly anyone bothers to ask who is dead when they hear a funeral bell.
175 *or ere*: before.

176 *nice*: accurate.

177–8 *That . . . one*: people mock the speaker who tells a tale that's an hour old because every minute brings ('teems' = breeds) a new one.
178 *does*: is.

182 *niggard*: miser.

Malcolm
I know him now. Good God betimes remove
165 The means that makes us strangers.
    Ross
                                        Sir, amen.
Macduff
Stands Scotland where it did?
    Ross
                                        Alas, poor country,
Almost afraid to know itself. It cannot
Be call'd our mother, but our grave, where nothing,
But who knows nothing, is once seen to smile;
170 Where sighs, and groans, and shrieks that rend the air
Are made, not mark'd; where violent sorrow seems
A modern ecstasy. The deadman's knell
Is there scarce ask'd for who, and good men's lives
Expire before the flowers in their caps,
175 Dying or ere they sicken.
    Macduff
                                O relation
Too nice, and yet too true.
    Malcolm
                                What's the newest grief?
    Ross
That of an hour's age doth hiss the speaker;
Each minute teems a new one.
    Macduff
                                How does my wife?
    Ross
Why, well.
    Macduff
                And all my children?
    Ross
                                        Well, too.
    Macduff
180 The tyrant has not batter'd at their peace?
    Ross
No, they were well at peace when I did leave 'em.
    Macduff
Be not a niggard of your speech: how goes't?

<table>
<tr><td>

183–90 *When . . . distresses*: Ross dodges Macduff's question about his family.

185 *out*: preparing for war.

186–7 *Which . . . afoot*: I had evidence to confirm my belief when I saw Macbeth's army on the move.
188 *eye*: presence in person.

190 *doff*: cast off (like clothes).

193–4 *An . . . out*: no soldier in the whole Christian kingdom is said to be a more experienced ('older') and better soldier.

196 *would be*: ought to be.
197 *latch*: catch.

198–9 *a fee-grief . . . breast*: very personal grief belonging to one person alone; Macduff uses legal terminology.

</td><td>

Ross

When I came hither to transport the tidings

Which I have heavily borne, there ran a rumour

185 Of many worthy fellows that were out,

Which was to my belief witness'd the rather

For that I saw the tyrant's power afoot.

Now is the time of help. [*To* Malcolm] Your eye in Scotland

Would create soldiers, make our women fight

190 To doff their dire distresses.

   Malcolm

                          Be't their comfort

We are coming thither. Gracious England hath

Lent us good Siward and ten thousand men—

An older and a better soldier none

That Christendom gives out.

   Ross

                        Would I could answer

195 This comfort with the like. But I have words

That would be howl'd out in the desert air,

Where hearing should not latch them.

   Macduff

                       What concern they?

The general cause, or is it a fee-grief

Due to some single breast?

   Ross

                    No mind that's honest

200 But in it shares some woe, though the main part

Pertains to you alone.

   Macduff

                If it be mine,

Keep it not from me; quickly let me have it.

   Ross

Let not your ears despise my tongue forever

Which shall possess them with the heaviest sound

205 That ever yet they heard.

   Macduff

               H'm—I guess at it.

   Ross

Your castle is surpris'd; your wife and babes

Savagely slaughter'd. To relate the manner

</td></tr>
</table>

208 *quarry . . . deer*: piled up bodies of
    deer killed in a day's hunting; Ross
    makes a bitter pun on 'deer' and
    'dear'.

210 *pull . . . brows*: Macduff is trying to
    hide his grief.
211–12 *the grief . . . break*: when grief
    doesn't speak out, it breaks the
    overburdened heart.

214 *from thence*: away from home.

218 *He has no children*: Macduff may refer
    either to Malcolm (who cannot know a
    father's feelings), or to Macbeth (who
    cannot be made to suffer appropriate
    revenge).
219 *hell-kite*: devilish bird of prey.
221 *one fell swoop*: a single savage attack;
    the now-proverbial phrase originated
    here.
222 *Dispute*: bear.
    like a man: i.e. bravely.
224 *as a man*: i.e. with grief.

228 *for thee*: because of you.
228–9 *Naught . . . demerits*: although I
    am nothing, they were killed because
    of my failings.

Were on the quarry of these murder'd deer
To add the death of you.

   Malcolm

                      Merciful heaven—

210 What, man, ne'er pull your hat upon your brows:
Give sorrow words; the grief that does not speak,
Whispers the o'erfraught heart and bids it break.

   Macduff

My children too?

   Ross

                 Wife, children, servants, all
That could be found.

   Macduff

                    And I must be from thence?

215 My wife kill'd too?

   Ross

                 I have said.

   Malcolm

                      Be comforted.
Let's make us med'cines of our great revenge
To cure this deadly grief.

   Macduff

He has no children. All my pretty ones?
Did you say all? O hell-kite! All?

220 What, all my pretty chickens and their dam
At one fell swoop?

   Malcolm

Dispute it like a man.

   Macduff

I shall do so;
But I must also feel it as a man;

225 I cannot but remember such things were
That were most precious to me. Did heaven look on,
And would not take their part? Sinful Macduff,
They were all struck for thee. Naught that I am,
Not for their own demerits but for mine,

230 Fell slaughter on their souls. Heaven rest them now.

   Malcolm

Be this the whetstone of your sword, let grief
Convert to anger. Blunt not the heart, enrage it.

233 *I . . . eyes*: I could act like a woman and weep.
234 *braggart*: boaster (threatening more than he can do).
235 *intermission*: interval (between now and the time he meets Macbeth). *Front to front*: face (forehead) to face.
237–8 *if . . . too*: may God forgive him also if I allow him to escape.

240 *leave*: permission to depart.

242 *put . . . instruments*: are arming themselves; Malcolm claims that the forces of good are on his side (just as Lady Macbeth invoked the powers of evil for the murder of Duncan).

Macduff
O, I could play the woman with mine eyes
And braggart with my tongue. But gentle heavens,
235 Cut short all intermission. Front to front
Bring thou this fiend of Scotland and myself;
Within my sword's length set him. If he scape,
Heaven forgive him too.
Malcolm
                                        This tune goes manly.
Come, go we to the king; our power is ready;
240 Our lack is nothing but our leave. Macbeth
Is ripe for shaking, and the powers above
Put on their instruments. Receive what cheer you may:
The night is long that never finds the day.   [*Exeunt*

'This is her very guise and, upon my life, fast asleep.' (*5*, 1, 17–18). Sara Kestelman as Lady Macbeth, Royal Shakespeare Company, 1982.

ACT 5

Act 5 Scene 1
Lady Macbeth walks in her sleep, dreaming about the murder of Duncan.

Os.d. *Doctor of Physic*: physician.

1 *watched*: stayed awake.

3 *field*: battlefield.
4 *night-gown*: dressing-gown (see 2, 2, 73).
5 *closet*: cabinet.
 fold: Elizabethans folded their writing-paper first to make margins then, after writing, to form envelopes.
6 *seal*: Letters were usually stamped over the folds with the writer's personal seal.
8 *perturbation*: disturbance.
9 *do . . . watching*: act as though she were awake.
10 *slumbery agitation*: sleeping activity; the Doctor's language is professionally formal.
11 *actual*: active, physical.
13 *report after her*: repeat behind her back.

16s.d. *taper*: candle.

17 *guise*: appearance.
18 *close*: hidden.

SCENE 1

Lady Macbeth's apartments: enter a Doctor of Physic, *and a* Waiting-Gentlewoman

Doctor
I have two nights watched with you, but can perceive no truth in your report. When was it she last walked?
Gentlewoman
Since his majesty went into the field, I have seen her rise from her bed, throw her night-gown upon her, unlock
5 her closet, take forth paper, fold it, write upon't, read it, afterwards seal it, and again return to bed, yet all this while in a most fast sleep.
Doctor
A great perturbation in nature, to receive at once the benefit of sleep and do the effects of watching. In this
10 slumbery agitation, besides her walking and other actual performances, what at any time have you heard her say?
Gentlewoman
That, sir, which I will not report after her.
Doctor
You may to me, and 'tis most meet you should.
Gentlewoman
15 Neither to you, nor anyone, having no witness to confirm my speech.

Enter Lady Macbeth, *with a taper*

Lo you, here she comes. This is her very guise and, upon my life, fast asleep. Observe her, stand close.
Doctor
How came she by that light?

Gentlewoman

20 Why, it stood by her. She has light by her continually, 'tis her command.

Doctor

You see her eyes are open.

Gentlewoman

Ay, but their sense are shut.

Doctor

What is it she does now? Look how she rubs her hands.

Gentlewoman

25 It is an accustomed action with her, to seem thus washing her hands; I have known her continue in this a quarter of an hour.

Lady Macbeth

Yet here's a spot.

Doctor

Hark, she speaks; I will set down what comes from her

30 to satisfy my remembrance the more strongly.

Lady Macbeth

Out, damned spot! Out, I say! One, two. Why then 'tis time to do't. Hell is murky. Fie, my lord, fie, a soldier, and afeard? What need we fear who knows it, when none can call our power to account? Yet who would

35 have thought the old man to have had so much blood in him?

Doctor

Do you mark that?

Lady Macbeth

The Thane of Fife had a wife. Where is she now? What, will these hands ne'er be clean? No more o'that, my

40 lord, no more o'that. You mar all with this starting.

Doctor

Go to, go to; you have known what you should not.

Gentlewoman

She has spoke what she should not, I am sure of that. Heaven knows what she has known.

Lady Macbeth

Here's the smell of the blood still; all the perfumes of

45 Arabia will not sweeten this little hand. O, O, O.

Doctor

What a sigh is there! The heart is sorely charged.

29 *set*: write.

31 *One, two*: Lady Macbeth, reliving her past experiences in her sleep, hears the striking of a bell—perhaps that which called Macbeth to murder Duncan (*2*, 1, 62).

34 *none . . . account*: there's no one who can challenge our authority.

38 *Thane of Fife*: Macduff.

40 *starting*: nervous jumpiness.

44–5 *perfumes of Arabia*: Many spices (from which perfumes were made) were imported from [Saudi] Arabia.

46 *sorely charged*: heavily burdened.

Gentlewoman

I would not have such a heart in my bosom for the dignity of the whole body.

Doctor

Well, well, well—

Gentlewoman

50 Pray God it be, sir.

Doctor

This disease is beyond my practice; yet I have known those which have walked in their sleep who have died holily in their beds.

Lady Macbeth

Wash your hands, put on your night-gown, look not so
55 pale. I tell you yet again, Banquo's buried; he cannot come out on's grave.

Doctor

Even so?

Lady Macbeth

To bed, to bed; there's knocking at the gate. Come, come, come, come, give me your hand; what's done
60 cannot be undone. To bed, to bed, to bed.   [*Exit*

Doctor

Will she go now to bed?

Gentlewoman

Directly.

Doctor

Foul whisp'rings are abroad; unnatural deeds
Do breed unnatural troubles; infected minds
65 To their deaf pillows will discharge their secrets.
More needs she the divine than the physician.
God, God forgive us all. Look after her;
Remove from her the means of all annoyance,
And still keep eyes upon her. So, good night,
70 My mind she has mated, and amaz'd my sight.
I think, but dare not speak.

Gentlewoman

Good night, good doctor.
                                                    [*Exeunt*

48 *dignity*: status (i.e. Lady Macbeth's status as queen).

51 *practice*: professional skill.

56 *on's*: of his.

63 *abroad*: about, at large.

66 *divine*: priest.

68 *means . . . annoyance*: anything she might use to harm herself.
69 *still*: always.
70 *mated*: stunned.
amaz'd: bewildered.

THIS PEN WILL STOP WORKING VERY VERY SOON

Act 5 Scene 2

A section of the army marches towards Dunsinane, and their leaders discuss the enemy, Macbeth, who is showing signs of panic.

0s.d. *Drum and colours*: military sounds and regimental banners.

1 *power*: force.

3 *Revenges*: desires for revenge.

3–5 *their . . . man*: those great causes would be enough to rouse a dead man to answer a call to arms in bloody warfare.

4 *bleeding*: bloodshed.

5 *mortified*: dead, insensible.

Scene 2

Countryside near Dunsinane. Drum and colours.
Enter Menteith, Caithness, Angus, Lennox, Soldiers

Menteith
The English power is near, led on by Malcolm,
His uncle Siward, and the good Macduff.
Revenges burn in them, for their dear causes
Would to the bleeding and the grim alarm
5   Excite the mortified man.

Angus
Near Birnam Wood
Shall we well meet them; that way are they coming.

Caithness
Who knows if Donaldbain be with his brother?

Lennox

For certain, sir, he is not. I have a file
Of all the gentry; there is Siward's son
10 And many unrough youths that even now
Protest their first of manhood.

Menteith

                                   What does the tyrant?

Caithness

Great Dunsinane he strongly fortifies.
Some say he's mad; others that lesser hate him
Do call it valiant fury, but for certain
15 He cannot buckle his distemper'd cause
Within the belt of rule.

Angus

                          Now does he feel
His secret murders sticking on his hands.
Now minutely revolts upbraid his faith-breach;
Those he commands, move only in command,
20 Nothing in love. Now does he feel his title
Hang loose about him, like a giant's robe
Upon a dwarfish thief.

Menteith

                        Who then shall blame
His pester'd senses to recoil and start
When all that is within him does condemn
25 Itself for being there?

Caithness

                          Well, march we on
To give obedience where 'tis truly ow'd;
Meet we the med'cine of the sickly weal,
And with him pour we in our country's purge,
Each drop of us.

Lennox

                  Or so much as it needs
30 To dew the sovereign flower and drown the weeds.
Make we our march towards Birnam.

                                   [*Exeunt, marching*

---

10 *unrough*: beardless.

11 *Protest . . . manhood*: show that now they have reached manhood.

15–16 *buckle . . . rule*: contain his disordered government through control by force.

18 *minutely . . . breach*: every minute new revolts reproach him for his own treason.

19–20 *move . . . love*: act in obedience only and not in loyalty.

20–2 *Now . . . thief*: Once again titles and ambitions are described in terms of clothing.

23 *pester'd*: vexed.

24–5 *all . . . there*: Macbeth's own nature is in rebellion against himself.

27 *med'cine*: physician—i.e. Malcolm. *weal*: land.

28–9 *pour . . . us*: pour out every drop of our blood to cleanse our country; blood-letting—drawing blood from a patient—was regularly used in the treatment of diseases.

30 *dew*: water.

Act 5 Scene 3
Macbeth learns of the approaching armies; he discusses his wife's condition with the Doctor, then goes off to battle.

1 *them*: the thanes.

3 *taint*: go rotten, lose courage.

5 *mortal consequences*: human fates.

8 *The English epicures*: the soft-living English.
9 *sway*: rule myself.

11 *cream-fac'd*: white-faced.
   loon: lound—a Scottish term of abuse (= villain, rogue).

14 *over-red*: redden over, paint red over.
15 *lily-liver'd*: with a bloodless liver (traditionally thought to be the seat of courage).
   patch: idiot.
17 *whey-face*: milk-face; 'whey' is the thin white liquid left when the milk curdles.

20 *push*: onslaught; thrust (of weapons).
21 *cheer*: comfort; Macbeth can still make a pun with 'chair'.
   disseat: unseat, de-throne.
22 *my way of life*: the course of my life.

Scene 3

Dunsinane, Macbeth's castle: enter Macbeth, Doctor, *and* Attendants

Macbeth
Bring me no more reports, let them fly all;
Till Birnam Wood remove to Dunsinane,
I cannot taint with fear. What's the boy Malcolm?
Was he not born of woman? The spirits that know
5 All mortal consequences have pronounc'd me thus:
'Fear not, Macbeth, no man that's born of woman
Shall e'er have power upon thee.' Then fly false thanes
And mingle with the English epicures;
The mind I sway by and the heart I bear
10 Shall never sag with doubt nor shake with fear.

Enter Servant

The devil damn thee black, thou cream-fac'd loon.
Where got'st thou that goose-look?
   Servant
There is ten thousand—
   Macbeth
                                Geese, villain?
   Servant
                                                Soldiers, sir.
   Macbeth
Go prick thy face and over-red thy fear,
15 Thou lily-liver'd boy. What soldiers, patch?
Death of thy soul, those linen cheeks of thine
Are counsellors to fear. What soldiers, whey-face?
   Servant
The English force, so please you.
   Macbeth
Take thy face hence!   [*Exit* Servant
                        Seyton!—I am sick at heart,
20 When I behold—Seyton, I say!—this push
Will cheer me ever or disseat me now.
I have liv'd long enough. My way of life

23 *the sere . . . leaf*: Compare the opening
   lines of Shakespeare's Sonnet 73,
   'That time of year thou mayst in me
   behold I When yellow leaves, or none,
   or few do hang I Upon those boughs
   that shake against the cold . . . '
   sere: dry, withered.
27 *mouth-honour*: flattery, lip-service.
28 *fain*: willingly.

Is fall'n into the sere, the yellow leaf,
And that which should accompany old age,
25 As honour, love, obedience, troops of friends,
I must not look to have; but in their stead,
Curses, not loud but deep, mouth-honour, breath
Which the poor heart would fain deny, and dare not.
Seyton!

Enter Seyton

Seyton
30 What's your gracious pleasure?
   Macbeth
                                        What news more?
   Seyton
All is confirm'd, my lord, which was reported.
   Macbeth
I'll fight till from my bones my flesh be hack'd.
Give me my armour.
   Seyton
'Tis not needed yet.
   Macbeth
35 I'll put it on;
   Send out more horses; skirr the country round.
   Hang those that talk of fear. Give me mine armour.
   How does your patient, doctor?
   Doctor
                                        Not so sick, my lord,
   As she is troubled with thick-coming fancies
40 That keep her from her rest.
   Macbeth
                                        Cure her of that.
   Canst thou not minister to a mind diseas'd,
   Pluck from the memory a rooted sorrow,
   Raze out the written troubles of the brain,
   And with some sweet oblivious antidote
45 Cleanse the stuff'd bosom of that perilous stuff
   Which weighs upon the heart?
   Doctor
                                        Therein the patient
   Must minister to himself.

36 *skirr*: scour.

39 *thick-coming*: coming in rapid
   succession.

41 *minister to*: treat.
42 *rooted*: deeply embedded.
43 *Raze*: eradicate, root out.
   written: imprinted.
44 *oblivious*: causing forgetfulness.
45 *stuff'd bosom*: burdened heart.

Macbeth
Throw physic to the dogs, I'll none of it.
Come, put mine armour on; give me my staff.—
50 Seyton, send out.—Doctor, the thanes fly from me.—
[*To* Attendant] Come sir, dispatch.—If thou couldst,
   doctor, cast
The water of my land, find her disease,
And purge it to a sound and pristine health,
I would applaud thee to the very echo
55 That should applaud again.—Pull't off, I say!—
What rhubarb, cynne, or what purgative drug
Would scour these English hence? Hear'st thou of
   them?
Doctor
Ay, my good lord; your royal preparation
Makes us hear something.
Macbeth
                  Bring it after me.—
60 I will not be afraid of death and bane,
Till Birnam Forest come to Dunsinane.
                  [*Exeunt all but* Doctor

Doctor
Were I from Dunsinane away and clear,
Profit again should hardly draw me here.   [*Exit*

SCENE 4

Birnam Wood. Drum and colours. Enter Malcolm,
Siward, Macduff, Siward's son, Menteith, Caithness,
Angus, *and* Soldiers, *marching*

Malcolm
Cousins, I hope the days are near at hand
That chambers will be safe.
Menteith
               We doubt it nothing.
Siward
What wood is this before us?
Menteith
                The Wood of Birnam.

---

51 *dispatch*: hurry up.
51–2 *cast The water*: test the urine.

53 *pristine*: undefiled.

55 *Pull't off*: Macbeth speaks to the attendant, probably referring to his armour.
56 *rhubarb, cynne*: medicinal plants prescribed as emetics and purgatives.
57 *scour*: drive out.
58 *preparation*: i.e. for war.

59 *Bring it after me*: Either the piece of armour of line 55, or some further news.
60 *bane*: destruction.

63 *Profit . . . here*: The avarice of physicians was always a target for satire.

Act 5 Scene 4
Malcolm's army camouflage themselves with branches from the trees of Birnam Wood.

2 *chambers . . . safe*: we shall be able to sleep in peace.

Malcolm

Let every soldier hew him down a bough,
5 And bear't before him; thereby shall we shadow
The numbers of our host and make discovery
Err in report of us.

A Soldier

It shall be done.

Siward

We learn no other, but the confident tyrant
Keeps still in Dunsinane and will endure
10 Our setting down before't.

Malcolm

'Tis his main hope,
For where there is advantage to be given,
Both more and less have given him the revolt,
And none serve with him but constrained things
Whose hearts are absent too.

Macduff

Let our just censures
15 Attend the true event and put we on
Industrious soldiership.

Siward

The time approaches
That will with due decision make us know
What we shall say we have and what we owe;
Thoughts speculative their unsure hopes relate,
20 But certain issue strokes must arbitrate.
Towards which, advance the war.   [*Exeunt, marching*

5 *shadow*: conceal.
6–7 *make . . . us*: make Macbeth's reconnaissance agents give a false report of our numbers.

8 *no other*: no other news.

10 *setting down*: laying siege, setting up camp.

11 *advantage . . . given*: opportunity to escape.
12 *more and less*: high and low in rank.
13 *constrained things*: constrainèd; miserable conscripts.
14–15 *Let . . . event*: let's leave our criticisms until the battle's over.

18 *owe*: lack, are missing.
19 *Thoughts . . . relate*: speculation about what will happen is based on uncertain hopes, but actual fighting ('strokes') will decide the certain outcome ('issue').

Act 5 Scene 5
When the battle is at its height, Macbeth learns that his wife has died—and that Birnam Wood is coming towards Dunsinane.

SCENE 5

Dunsinane: inside Macbeth's *castle; enter* Macbeth, Seyton, *and* Soldiers, *with drum and colours*

Macbeth
Hang out our banners on the outward walls;
The cry is still, 'They come.' Our castle's strength
Will laugh a siege to scorn; here let them lie
Till famine and the ague eat them up.

5 Were they not forc'd with those that should be ours,
We might have met them dareful, beard to beard,
And beat them backward home.

4 *ague*: disease (characterized by fever and shivering fits).
5 *forc'd*: reinforced.

A cry within of women

What is that noise?

Seyton
It is the cry of women, my good lord.

7s.d. *A cry within*: Some editors/directors send Seyton to enquire about this 'cry' ('*within*' = offstage); others introduce a servant who speaks to Seyton.

Macbeth
I have almost forgot the taste of fears;
10 The time has been, my senses would have cool'd
To hear a night-shriek and my fell of hair
Would at a dismal treatise rouse and stir
As life were in't. I have supp'd full with horrors;
Direness familiar to my slaughterous thoughts
15 Cannot once start me. Wherefore was that cry?

Seyton
The queen, my lord, is dead.

11 *fell*: head, shock.
12 *dismal treatise*: frightening story.
13 *As*: as if.
14 *Direness*: horror.
15 *start*: startle, alarm.

Macbeth
She should have died hereafter;
There would have been a time for such a word.
Tomorrow, and tomorrow, and tomorrow
Creeps in this petty pace from day to day
20 To the last syllable of recorded time;
And all our yesterdays have lighted fools
The way to dusty death. Out, out, brief candle,
Life's but a walking shadow, a poor player
That struts and frets his hour upon the stage
25 And then is heard no more. It is a tale

16–17 *She . . . word*: At least two meanings are possible for these lines: a) 'she would have died sooner or later: such a time would inevitably have come'; b) 'she ought to have died later, when there would have been more time (for mourning)'.
19 *petty*: trivial.
20 *To . . . time*: until the last syllable of remembered time shall have been recorded.
22 *candle*: i.e. life.
23 *player*: actor.
24 *frets*: raves.

Told by an idiot, full of sound and fury
Signifying nothing.

Enter a Messenger

Thou com'st to use thy tongue: thy story quickly.
Messenger
Gracious my lord,
30 I should report that which I say I saw,
But know not how to do't.
Macbeth
                                    Well, say, sir.
Messenger
As I did stand my watch upon the hill
I look'd toward Birnam and anon methought
The wood began to move.
Macbeth
                                    Liar and slave!
Messenger
35 Let me endure your wrath if't be not so;
Within this three mile may you see it coming.
I say, a moving grove.
Macbeth
                                    If thou speak'st false,
Upon the next tree shall thou hang alive
Till famine cling thee; if thy speech be sooth,
40 I care not if thou dost for me as much.
I pull in resolution and begin
To doubt th'equivocation of the fiend
That lies like truth. 'Fear not, till Birnam Wood
Do come to Dunsinane', and now a wood
45 Comes toward Dunsinane. Arm, arm, and out!
If this which he avouches does appear,
There is nor flying hence nor tarrying here.
I 'gin to be aweary of the sun
And wish th'estate o'th'world were now undone.
50 Ring the alarum bell! Blow wind, come wrack;
At least we'll die with harness on our back.   [*Exeunt*

30 *I say I saw*: The Messenger cannot believe his eyes.

32 *watch*: guard.
33 *anon*: suddenly.

39 *cling thee*: shrivel you up.
    sooth: truth, true.
41 *pull in resolution*: check my determination.
42 *equivocation*: double-dealing.
    fiend: i.e. the third Apparition.

46 *avouches*: claims, affirms.
47 *nor . . . nor*: neither . . . nor.
    tarrying: staying.
49 *estate o'th'world*: the order of creation.
51 *harness*: armour.

Act 5 Scene 6
Malcolm's army reaches Macbeth's castle:
battle is commenced.

Scene 6

*Dunsinane, surrounding the castle. Drum and
colours. Enter Malcolm, Siward, Macduff, and their
army, with boughs*

Malcolm
Now near enough; your leafy screens throw down
And show like those you are. You, worthy uncle,
Shall with my cousin your right noble son
Lead our first battle. Worthy Macduff and we
5 Shall take upon's what else remains to do,
According to our order.
    Siward
                         Fare you well.
Do we but find the tyrant's power tonight,
Let us be beaten if we cannot fight.
    Macduff
Make all our trumpets speak; give them all breath,
10 Those clamorous harbingers of blood and death.
                               [*Exeunt*

Alarums continued

4 *battle*: army, division of an army.
   we: Malcolm begins to speak in the
   royal plural.

7 *power*: military forces.

9 *give . . . breath*: blow them as hard as
   you can.
10 *harbingers*: officers sent ahead to
   make reservations (see *1, 4, 45*).
10s.d. *Alarums continued*: From this
   point onwards the action is
   continuous, and the audience must
   move in imagination to different parts
   of the battlefield.

Act 5 Scene 7
Macbeth encounters Young Siward and kills him.

SCENE 7

Before or inside the castle of Dunsinane: enter
Macbeth

Macbeth
They have tied me to a stake; I cannot fly,
But bear-like I must fight the course. What's he
That was not born of woman? Such a one
Am I to fear, or none.

Enter Young Siward

1 *tied . . . stake*: i.e. like a bear chained to a post and attacked by dogs in the so-called 'sport' of bear-baiting.

Young Siward
5 What is thy name?
    Macbeth
Thou'lt be afraid to hear it.
    Young Siward
No, though thou call'st thyself a hotter name
Than any is in hell.
    Macbeth
                 My name's Macbeth.
    Young Siward
The devil himself could not pronounce a title
10 More hateful to mine ear.
    Macbeth
                    No, nor more fearful.
    Young Siward

11 *abhorred*: abhorrèd.

Thou liest, abhorred tyrant; with my sword
I'll prove the lie thou speak'st.

Fight, and Young Siward *slain*

Macbeth
                    Thou wast born of woman.
But swords I smile at, weapons laugh to scorn,
Brandish'd by man that's of a woman born.
             [*Exit with* Young Siward'*s body*

Alarums. Enter Macduff

Macduff

15 That way the noise is. Tyrant, show thy face!
   If thou be'st slain, and with no stroke of mine,
   My wife and children's ghosts will haunt me still.
   I cannot strike at wretched kerns whose arms
   Are hir'd to bear their staves; either thou, Macbeth,
20 Or else my sword with an unbatter'd edge
   I sheath again undeeded. There thou shouldst be;
   By this great clatter, one of greatest note
   Seems bruited. Let me find him, Fortune,
   And more I beg not.   [*Exit*

Alarums. Enter Malcolm *and* Siward

Siward

25 This way, my lord; the castle's gently render'd.
   The tyrant's people on both sides do fight;
   The noble thanes do bravely in the war.
   The day almost itself professes yours,
   And little is to do.
      Malcolm
                     We have met with foes
30 That strike beside us.
      Siward
                        Enter, sir, the castle.   [*Exeunt*

Alarum

17 *still*: for ever.
18 *kerns*: lightly-armed foot-soldiers (see 1, 2, 13).
19 *staves*: lances.
   either thou: either I fight with you.
21 *undeeded*: having done nothing.
   There: that's where.
23 *bruited*: noised, reported.
25 *gently render'd*: surrendered without fuss.
30 *strike beside us*: who fight on our side.

Act 5 Scene 8
Macbeth encounters Macduff.

SCENE 8

Dunsinane: enter Macbeth

Macbeth
Why should I play the Roman fool and die
On mine own sword? Whiles I see lives, the gashes
Do better upon them.

1–2 *play . . . sword*: Roman honour demanded suicide rather than surrender.
2 *lives*: living men.

Enter Macduff

Macduff
                    Turn, hell-hound, turn.
Macbeth
Of all men else I have avoided thee,
5 But get thee back, my soul is too much charg'd
With blood of thine already.
Macduff
                    I have no words;
My voice is in my sword, thou bloodier villain
Than terms can give thee out.

5 *charg'd*: burdened.

8 *terms*: words, expressions.

Fight. Alarum

Macbeth
                    Thou losest labour.
As easy mayst thou the intrenchant air
10 With thy keen sword impress as make me bleed.
Let fall thy blade on vulnerable crests;
I bear a charmed life which must not yield
To one of woman born.
Macduff
                    Despair thy charm,
And let the angel whom thou still hast serv'd
15 Tell thee, Macduff was from his mother's womb
Untimely ripp'd.
Macbeth
Accursed be that tongue that tells me so,
For it hath cow'd my better part of man;
And be these juggling fiends no more believ'd
20 That palter with us in a double sense,

9 *intrenchant*: incapable of being cut.
10 *impress*: make a mark on.

12 *charmed*: charmèd.

14 *angel*: guiding spirit, the 'genius' referred to in *3, 1, 57–8*.
15–16 *from . . . ripped*: delivered prematurely by Caesarean section.

17 *Accursed*: accursèd.
18 *cow'd*: depressed, disheartened.
my . . . of man: the greater proportion of my courage.
20 *palter . . . sense*: trick us with double meanings.

21-2 *keep . . . hope*: keep their promises as we hear them but not as we hope for them.

24 *show and gaze*: spectacular exhibit.

26 *Painted . . . pole*: painted on a sign hung from a pole (as in a fair or carnival).

29 *baited*: taunted.

31 *oppos'd*: opposite me.
32 *try the last*: have a final attempt.

That keep the word of promise to our ear
And break it to our hope. I'll not fight with thee.
    Macduff
Then yield thee coward,
And live to be the show and gaze o'th'time.
25 We'll have thee, as our rarer monsters are,
Painted upon a pole and underwrit,
'Here may you see the tyrant.'
    Macbeth
                      I will not yield
To kiss the ground before young Malcolm's feet
And to be baited with the rabble's curse.
30 Though Birnam Wood be come to Dunsinane
And thou oppos'd being of no woman born,
Yet I will try the last. Before my body,
I throw my warlike shield. Lay on, Macduff,
And damn'd be him that first cries, 'Hold, enough!'
                      [*Exeunt, fighting. Alarums*

Enter Macbeth *and* Macduff, *fighting, and* Macbeth *slain*

        [*Exit* Macduff, *with* Macbeth's *body*

Act 5 Scene 9
Malcolm is proclaimed King.

0s.d. *flourish*: trumpet call to herald Malcolm's approach.

1 *we miss*: who are missing.

2 *go off*: be killed.
by these: judging by these men I see here.

5 *soldier's debt*: what a soldier owes—i.e. his life.
8 *the . . . fought*: the position where he fought without flinching.

10–12 *Your . . . end*: you must not measure your grief by his worth, because then it would be endless.

12 *before*: in the front of his body; see '*Macbeth*: the source', p.101.

15 *hairs*: the hairs on my head (a proverbial comparison); perhaps Siward makes a pun with 'heirs'.
17 *knell*: funeral bell (see *2, 1, 63*).

19 *score*: debt—see line 5.

SCENE 9

Malcolm's headquarters. Retreat, and flourish. Enter with drum and colours, Malcolm, Siward, Ross, Thanes, and Soldiers

Malcolm
I would the friends we miss were safe arriv'd.
    Siward
Some must go off. And yet by these I see,
So great a day as this is cheaply bought.
    Malcolm
Macduff is missing and your noble son.
    Ross
5 Your son, my lord, has paid a soldier's debt;
He only liv'd but till he was a man,
The which no sooner had his prowess confirm'd
In the unshrinking station where he fought,
But like a man he died.
    Siward
                    Then he is dead?
    Ross
10 Ay, and brought off the field. Your cause of sorrow
Must not be measur'd by his worth, for then
It hath no end.
    Siward
                Had he his hurts before?
    Ross
Ay, on the front.
    Siward
Why then, God's soldier be he;
15 Had I as many sons as I have hairs,
I would not wish them to a fairer death.
And so his knell is knoll'd.
    Malcolm
                  He's worth more sorrow,
And that I'll spend for him.
    Siward
                  He's worth no more;
They say he parted well and paid his score,
20 And so God be with him. Here comes newer comfort.

Enter Macduff, *with* Macbeth's *head*

Macduff

Hail, king, for so thou art. Behold where stands
Th'usurper's cursed head. The time is free.
I see thee compass'd with thy kingdom's pearl,
That speak my salutation in their minds;
25 Whose voices I desire aloud with mine.
Hail, King of Scotland.

All

Hail, King of Scotland.

Flourish

Malcolm

We shall not spend a large expense of time
Before we reckon with your several loves
And make us even with you. My thanes and kinsmen,
30 Henceforth be earls, the first that ever Scotland
In such an honour nam'd. What's more to do
Which would be planted newly with the time,—
As calling home our exil'd friends abroad
That fled the snares of watchful tyranny,
35 Producing forth the cruel ministers
Of this dead butcher and his fiend-like queen,
Who, as 'tis thought, by self and violent hands
Took off her life,—this and what needful else
That calls upon us, by the grace of Grace
40 We will perform in measure, time, and place.
So, thanks to all at once and to each one,
Whom we invite to see us crown'd at Scone.

Flourish

[*Exeunt*

22 *cursed*: cursèd.
23 *compass'd with*: surrounded by.
pearl: jewels—i.e. the thanes.

26s.d. *Flourish*: fanfare.

28 *reckon*: settle accounts.
several: separate, individual.

32 *would . . . time*: ought to be started now, just as a new age has begun; Malcolm's gardening metaphor seems to echo Duncan's words, *1*, 4, 28–9.

37 *self . . . hands*: her own violent hands.

39 *calls upon us*: demands our attention.
Grace: god.
40 *in measure . . . place*: in the correct order, at the right time, and in the proper place: Malcolm restores harmony to Scotland.
42 *Scone*: The traditional site of Scottish coronations; compare *2*, 4, 31.

Macbeth: the source

Shakespeare's main source for *Macbeth* was *The Chronicles of Scotland*, which was compiled by Raphael Holinshed in 1577 and which provided a complete outline of Macbeth's career from his first meeting with the witches until his death at the hands of Macduff. The murder of King Duncan was amplified by further details from Holinshed's account of the killing of an earlier Scottish king, King Duff, who was also murdered when he was the guest of a trusted subject. The following passages are extracts from the *Chronicles*, with modernized spelling and punctuation; dots (. . .) indicate that something has been missed out, and in order to make a continuous narrative some words have been inserted and are indicated by square brackets [. . .].

It fortuned as Macbeth and Banquo journeyed towards Forres . . . there met them three women in strange and wild apparel . . . The first of them spake and said, 'All hail, Macbeth, Thane of Glamis.' (For he had lately entered into that dignity and office by the death of his father Sinel.) The second of them said, 'All hail, Macbeth, Thane of Cawdor.' But the third said 'All hail, Macbeth, that hereafter shalt be King of Scotland.'

Then Banquo: 'What manner of women' (said he) 'are you, that seem so little favourable unto me, whereas to my fellow here, besides high offices, ye assign also the Kingdom, appointing further nothing for me at all?'

'Yes' (says the first of them) 'we promise greater benefits unto thee than unto him, for he shall reign indeed, but with an unlucky end; neither shall he leave any issue behind him to succeed in his place, where contrarily thou indeed shall not reign at all, but of thee those shall be born which shall govern the Scottish Kingdom by long order of continual descent.'

Herewith the aforesaid women vanished immediately out of their sight . . . The common opinion was that these women were either the weird sisters . . . or else some nymphs or fairies . . .

Shortly after, the Thane of Cawdor being condemned at Forres of treason against the king committed, his lands, livings and offices were given of the king's liberality to Macbeth.

The same night after, at supper, Banquo jested with him and said, 'Now, Macbeth, thou has obtained those things which the two former sisters prophesied, there remaineth only for thee to purchase that which the third said should come to pass.'

Whereupon Macbeth, revolving the thing in his mind, began even then to devise how he might attain to the kingdom; but yet he thought with himself that he must tarry a time, which should advance him thereto (by the divine providence) as it had come to pass in his former preferment. But shortly after it chanced that King Duncan, having two sons . . . he made the elder of them called Malcolm, Prince of Cumberland, as it were thereby to appoint him his successor in the kingdom immediately after his decease. Macbeth [was] sore troubled therewith [and] he began to take counsel how he might usurp the kingdom by force . . .

The words of the three sisters . . . greatly encouraged him hereunto, but specially his wife lay sore upon him to attempt the thing, as she that was very ambitious, burning in unquenchable desire to bear the name of queen. At length therefore . . . he slew the king . . . [and then] he caused himself to be proclaimed king, and forthwith went unto Scone, where . . . he received the investiture of the kingdom according to the accustomed manner.

Malcolm . . . and Donald Bane, the sons of King Duncan, for fear of their lives (which they might well know that Macbeth would seek to bring to an end for his more sure confirmation in the estate) fled into Cumberland, where Malcolm remained, till time that [King] Edward . . . received [him] by way of most friendly entertainment; but Donald passed over into Ireland where he was tenderly cherished by the king of that land . . .

Macbeth govern[ed] the realm for a space of ten years in equal justice . . . [but then] he began to show what he was . . . For the prick of conscience . . . caused him ever to fear, lest he should be served by the same cup as he had administered to his predecessor.

The words also of the three weird sisters would not out of his mind, which as they had promised him the kingdom, so likewise did they promise it at the same time unto the heirs of Banquo. He willed, therefore, the same Banquo with his son named Fleance, to come to [a] supper that he had prepared for them—which was indeed, as he had devised, present death at the hands of certain murderers. [He had hired these men] to execute that deed, appointing them to meet with that same Banquo and his son without the palace, as they returned to their lodgings, and there to slay them . . . it chanced yet by benefit of the dark night, that although the father were slain, the son . . . escaped that danger . . .

After the contrived slaughter of Banquo, nothing prospered with the foresaid Macbeth: for in manner every man began to doubt his own life … And even as there were many that stood in fear of him, so likewise stood he in fear of many …

[Macbeth] had learned of certain wizards … that he ought to take heed of Macduff, who in time to come should seek to destroy him. And surely hereupon had he put Macduff to death, but that a certain witch, whom he had in great trust, had told [him] that he should never be slain with man born of any woman, nor vanquished till the wood of Birnam came in[to] the castle of Dunsinane. By this prophecy Macbeth put all fear out of his heart, supposing that he might do what he would …

At length Macduff, to avoid peril of life, purposed with himself to pass into England, to procure Malcolm to claim the crown of Scotland. But this was not so secretly devised by Macduff, but that Macbeth had knowledge given him thereof … for Macbeth had in every nobleman's house one sly fellow or other in fee with him, to reveal all that was said or done within the same … Immediately then, being advertised whereabout Macduff went, he came hastily with a great power unto Fife, and forthwith besieged the castle where Macduff dwelt, trusting to have found him therein … Macbeth most cruelly caused the wife and children of Macduff, with all other whom he found in that castle, to be slain. Also he confiscated the goods of Macduff [and] proclaimed him traitor …

But Macduff was already escaped out of danger and gotten into England … [and] at his coming unto Malcolm, he declared into what great misery the estate of Scotland was brought, by the detestable cruelties exercised by the tyrant Macbeth.

Malcolm, hearing Macduff's words … fetched a deep sigh. [Macduff urged Malcolm to return and claim the crown of Scotland, but,] though Malcolm was very sorrowful for the oppression of his countrymen the Scots, in manner as Macduff had declared, yet doubting whether he would come as one that meant unfeignedly as he spake, or else as sent from Macbeth to betray him, he thought to have some further trial, and thereupon dissembling his mind at the first, he answered as follows:

'I am truly very sorry for the misery chanced to my country of Scotland, but though I have never so great affection to relieve the same, I am nothing meet thereto. First, such immoderate lust and voluptuous sensuality … followeth me, that if I were made King of Scots, I should seek to deflower your maids and matrons, in such wise that mine intemperance should be no more importable unto you than the bloody tyranny of Macbeth now is.' Hereunto Macduff answered, 'This surely is a very evil fault, for many noble princes and kings have lost both lives and kingdoms for the same; nevertheless, there are women ennow in Scotland . . .'

Then said Malcolm, 'I am also the most avaricious creature on the earth, so that if I were king, I should seek so many ways to get lands and goods, that I would slay the most part of all the nobles of Scotland to the end . . . that I might enjoy their lands, goods, and possessions . . .' Macduff to this made answer, how it was a far worse fault than the other: for avarice is the root of all mischief . . . 'Yet notwithstanding, follow my counsel, and take upon thee the crown. There is gold and riches enough in Scotland to satisfy thy greedy desire.'

Then said Malcolm again, 'I am further inclined to dissimulation, telling of leasings and all other kinds of deceit . . . Then sith there is nothing that more becometh a prince than constancy, verity, truth, and justice, with the other laudable fellowship of those fair and noble virtues . . . you see how unable I am to govern any province or region . . .'

Then said Macduff, 'This is the worst of all, and there I leave thee, and therefore say, "Oh ye unhappy and miserable Scottishmen . . . ye have one cursed and wicked tyrant that now reigneth over you, without any right or title . . . The other, that hath the right to the crown, is . . . nothing worthy to enjoy it ever" ' . . .

At the last, when he was ready to depart, Malcolm took him by the sleeve and said, 'Be of good comfort, Macduff, for I have none of these vices before remembered, but have jested with thee in this manner only to prove thy mind. For diverse times heretofore hath Macbeth sought by this manner of means to bring me into his hands . . .'

[Then Macduff returned to Scotland, and called the nobles of the realm to assist Malcolm to reclaim the throne.]

In the meantime, Malcolm purchased such favour at King Edward's hands, that old Siward, Earl of Northumberland, was appointed, with ten thousand men, to go with him into Scotland to support him in this enterprise for recovery of his right . . . After that Macbeth perceived his enemies' power to increase . . . he recoiled back into Fife, there purposing to abide in camp fortified at the castle of Dunsinane, and to fight with his enemies if they meant to pursue him . . . He had such confidence in his prophecies, that he believed that he should never be vanquished, till Birnam Wood be brought to Dunsinane, nor yet to be slain with any that should be or was born of any woman.

Malcolm, following hastily after Macbeth, came the night before the battle unto Birnam Wood, and when his army had rested a while there to refresh them, he commanded every man to get a bough of some tree or other of that wood in his hand, as big as he might bear, and to march forth therewith in such wise that on the next morrow they might come closely and without sight in this manner within view of his enemies.

On the morrow, when Macbeth beheld them coming in this sort, [he] first marvelled what the matter meant, but in the end remembered himself that the prophecy which he had heard long time before that time, of the coming of Birnam Wood to Dunsinane Castle was likely to be fulfilled. Nevertheless, he brought his men in order of battle, and exhorted them to do valiantly. Howbeit, his enemies had scarcely cast from them their boughs when Macbeth, perceiving their numbers, betook him straight to flight . . .

[Macduff pursued Macbeth, who challenged him], saying, 'Thou traitor, what meaneth it that thou shouldst thus in vain follow me, that am not appointed to be slain by any creature that is born of a woman. Come on, therefore . . . ' But Macduff . . . answered (with his naked sword in his hand), saying, 'It is true, Macbeth . . . for I am even he that thy wizards have told thee of, who was never born of my mother, but ripped out of her womb.' Therewithal he stepped unto [Macbeth], and slew him in the place. Then cutting his head from his shoulders he set it upon a pole and brought it unto Malcolm.

Malcolm . . . thus recovering the realm . . . was crowned at Scone . . . Immediately after his coronation, he called a parliament . . . in which he rewarded them in lands and in livings that had assisted him against Macbeth . . . He created many earls . . . [and] these were the first earls that have ever been heard of amongst the Scottishmen . . .

Earl Siward [had] sent his son [into Scotland] with an army to conquer the land, whose hap was there to be slain. When his father heard the news he demanded whether he received the wounds whereof he died in the fore-part of his body, or in the hinder-part: and when it was told him that he received it in the fore-part, 'I rejoice' (saith he) 'even with all my heart, for I would not wish either to my son nor to my self any other kind of death.'

Donwald murders King Duff

[After some of his kinsmen had been put to death for treason, Donwald, the 'captain of the castle' at Forres], conceived such an inward malice toward the king . . . [and] through setting of his wife . . . he found means to murder the king within the aforesaid castle of Forres . . . For the king, being in that country, was accustomed to lie most commonly within the same castle, having special trust in Donwald, as a man whom he never suspected . . .

[Donwald still held a grudge against the King], which his wife, perceiving, ceased not to travail with him until she understood the cause of his displeasure. Which at length when she had learned by his own relation, she, as one that bear no less malice in her heart towards the king . . . counselled him . . . to make him away, and showed him the means whereby he might soonest accomplish it. Donwald thus being the more kindled in wrath by the words of his wife, determined to follow her advice in the execution of so heinous an act. Whereupon devising with himself for a while, which way he might best accomplish his accursed intent, [he] at length got opportunity, and sped his purpose as followeth.

It chanced that the king, upon the day before he purposed to depart forth of the castle . . . called such afore him as had faithfully served him in pursuit and apprehension of the rebels; and, giving them hearty thanks, he bestowed sundry honourable gifts amongst them. Of the which number Donwald was one, as he that had been ever accounted a most faithful servant to the king.

At length . . . he got him into his privy chamber, only with two of his chamberlains. [These men], having brought [the king] to bed, came forth again, and then fell to banqueting with Donwald and his wife . . . Whereat they sat up so long, till they had charged their stomachs with such full gorges that their heads were no sooner got to the pillow, but asleep they were—so fast that a man might have removed the chamber over them, sooner than to have waked them out of their drunken sleep.

[Donwald persuaded some of his servants to murder the king and carry his body out of the castle.]

Donwald, about the time that the murder was doing, got him amongst them that kept the watch, and so continued to company with them all the residue of the night. But in the morning when the noise was raised in the king's chamber of how the king was slain . . . he with the watch ran thither, as though he had known nothing of the matter, and breaking into the chamber, and finding cakes of blood in the bed, and on the floor about the sides of it, he forthwith slew the chamberlains as guilty of that heinous murder . . .

Finally, such was his over earnest diligence in the severe inquisition and trial of the offenders herein, that some of the lords began to mislike the matter, and to smell forth shrewd tokens, that he should not be altogether clear himself . . .

For the space of six months together, after this heinous murder thus committed, there appeared no sun by day, nor moon by night in any part of the realm, but still was the sky covered in continual clouds, and sometimes such outrageous winds arose, with lightnings and tempests, that the people were in great fear of present destruction . . .

Monstrous sights also that were seen in the Scottish kingdom that year were these: horses in Lothian, being of singular beauty and swiftness, did eat their own flesh . . . there was also a sparhawk strangled by an owl . . .

Songs from *The Witch* by Thomas Middleton

The play must have been revised or adapted at some time before publication of the Folio edition in 1623, which gives additional opportunities and songs to the Witches (whose numbers were augmented for the entertainment).

1 **Act 3, Scene 5, line 33**

Sing within

First Witch	Come away Heccat, Heccat, Oh, come away.
Second Witch	I come, I come, with all the speed I may,
	I come, I come, with all the speed I may.
First Witch	Where's Stadling?
Third Witch	Here.
First Witch	Where's Puckle?
Fourth Witch	Here, and Hopper too, and Helway too.
First Witch	We want but you, we want but you.
	Come away, make up the count,
	I will but noint, and then I mount.　　*noint:* anoint myself
	I will, &c.
First Witch	Here comes one, it is
	To fetch his due, a kiss,
	Ay, a cull, sip of blood;　　　　　　　　*cull:* embrace
	And why thou stayst so long, I muse,
	Since the air's so sweet and good.
	Oh art thou come! What news?
Second Witch	All goes fair for our delight,
	Either come, or else refuse.

Now I am furnished for the flight,
Now I go, now I fly.
Malkin my sweet spirit and I.

Third Witch   Oh what a dainty pleasure's this,
To sail i'th'air,
While the moon shines fair,
To sing, to toy and kiss,   *toy*: play
Over woods, high rocks and mountains,
Over misty hills and fountains,
Over steeples, towers and turrets,
We fly by night 'mongst troops of spirits.

Chorus   No ring of bells to our ears sounds,
No howls of wolves, nor yelp of hounds,
No, nor the noise of waters breach,   *breach*: breaking
Nor cannons' throats our height can reach.

2   Act 4, Scene 1, line 43

Black spirits, and white; red spirits, and gray,
Mingle, mingle, mingle; you that mingle may.
    Titty, Tiffin, keep it stiff in.
    Fire-Drake, Pucky, make it lucky.
    Liand, Robin, you must bob in.
Round, a-round, a-round, about, about
    All ill come running in, all good keep out.

First Witch   Here's the blood of a bat.
Hecate   Put in that; oh put in that.
Second Witch   Here's libbard's bane.   *libbard*: leopard
Hecate   Put in again.
First Witch   The juice of toad, the oil of adder.
Second Witch   That will make the younker madder.   *younker*: fellow
Hecate   Put in: there's all, and rid the stench.
Firestone   Nay, here's three ounces of the red-haired wench.
All   Round: around, around, &c.

Classwork and Examinations

The plays of Shakespeare are studied all over the world, and this classroom edition is being used in many different countries. Teaching methods vary from school to school—even *within* the United Kingdom—and there are many different ways of examining a student's work. Some teachers and examiners expect detailed knowledge of Shakespeare's text; others ask for imaginative involvement with his characters and their situations; and there are some teachers who want their students, by means of 'workshop' activities, to share in the theatrical experience of directing and performing a play. Most people use a variety of methods. This section of the book offers a few suggestions for approaches to *Macbeth* which could be used in schools and colleges to help with students' understanding and *enjoyment* of the play.

A Discussion of Themes and Topics
B Character Study
C Activities
D Context Questions
E Critical Appreciation
F Essays
G Projects

A Discussion of Themes and Topics

Talking about the play—about the issues it raises and the characters who are involved—is one of the most rewarding and pleasurable aspects of the study of Shakespeare. It is most sensible to discuss each scene as it is read, sharing impressions (and perhaps correcting misapprehensions): no two people experience any character in quite the same way, and we all have different expectations. It can be useful to compare aspects of this play with other fictions—plays, novels, films— or with modern life. A large class can divide into small groups, each with a leader, who can discuss different aspects of a single topic and then report back to the main assembly.

Suggestions

A1 The play opens with three witches. How would you present this scene so that a modern audience is properly impressed?

A2 Speaking of her husband, Lady Macbeth says:

> Thou would'st be great,
> Art not without ambition, but without
> The illness should attend it;

1, 5, 17–19

What do you think she means by this? Is it not possible to be ambitious—and successful—without some kind of 'illness'?

A3   When he welcomes the king to his castle, Macbeth describes what he believes to be the duty of a loyal subject:

> ... our duties
> Are to your throne and state, children and servants,
> Which do but what they should by doing everything
> Safe toward your love and honour.   *1, 4, 24–7*

How would *you* describe the duty of a subject, or citizen, today? What loyalties are important in your school life?

A4   At the banquet in *Act 3*, Scene 4, Macbeth sees the ghost of the murdered Banquo. How would you present this scene?

A5   Is the Porter's scene really necessary?

A6   Do these witches in fact have any power?

A7   In order to test Macduff, Malcolm describes himself as the complete opposite of an ideal king (4, 3, 50–100). What in your view are the qualities that would make a good ruler (king, president, prime minister, head teacher)?

A8   What is your idea of a tyrant?

A9   Does the 'sleepwalking' scene (*Act 5*, Scene 1) cause you to feel sorry for Lady Macbeth?

A10   Is Macbeth a hero or a villain?

B Character Study   Shakespeare's characters can be studied in many different ways, either from the *outside*, where the detached, critical student (or group of students) can see the function of every character within the whole scheme and pattern of the play; or from the *inside*, where the sympathetic student (like an actor) can identify with a single character and can look at the action and the other characters from his/her point of view.

Suggestions   a) from 'outside' the character

B1   What is your impression of Macbeth after reading *Act 1*, Scene 2? How is this first impression modified as the play progresses?

B2   Describe the character of Lady Macbeth before the murder of Duncan. Is she more or less guilty than her husband?

B3   Compare the character of Shakespeare's Duncan with that of Holinshed's King of Scotland. Why do you think that Shakespeare made such changes to the character?

B4   Can you suggest any reason for the presence of the Third Murderer?

B5   Do you find Macduff a sympathetic character?

b) from 'inside' the character

B6   Macbeth wrote to tell his wife about the meeting with the witches. Write a letter from Banquo to his wife, describing the same encounter.

B7   As one of the lords attending the king, write to your wife and describe your arrival at the castle of Macbeth, and the welcome with which you were received.

B8   The Porter was present when the murder of Duncan was revealed. How would he describe the scene to his pals in the pub?

B9   What are the thoughts that pass through Macbeth's mind as he waits for his crime to be revealed? Write a 'stream-of-consciousness' account of the second part—lines 45ff—of *Act* 2, Scene 3.

B10   After the murder is discovered, both Malcolm and Donaldbain flee from Scotland to ask for political asylum in (respectively) England and Ireland. How would they explain their need for refuge?

B11   In the character of one of those present at Macbeth's great feast—a Lord, Lady, or Servant—tell your friends all about it.

B12   Lady Macbeth has no one to talk to—perhaps she confides in her diary? Write the entry describing her husband's strange behaviour, and her own attempts to 'cover up' for him, at the banquet in *Act 3*, Scene 4.

B13   Suppose Lady Macduff had time to write a letter, either to her husband or to a friend, before she was interrupted by the murderers in *Act 4*, Scene 2. How would she write of her love and loyalty for her husband, and her fears for herself and her children?

B14   'A remarkable case of somnambulism': Lady Macbeth's Doctor writes the case history for a medical journal.

B15 In *Act 5*, Scene 3, both the Servant and the Doctor are terrified. In the character of either, describe the situation to your friends/colleagues—or to newspaper/TV reporters.

B16 Write Macbeth's memoirs (discovered after his death) describing the last days in Dunsinane.

C Activities These can involve two or more students, preferably working away from the desk or study-table. They can help students to develop a sense of drama and the dramatic aspects of Shakespeare's play—which was written to be spoken and performed, not read silently.

Suggestions **C1** Act the play, or at least part of it. You don't need scenery or properties—just space and people.

C2 Speak the soliloquies of Macbeth *in your own words.*

C3 'We will speak further' (*1*, 5, 70). Plan a scene between Macbeth and Lady Macbeth before the king's visit to their castle.

C4 Macbeth twice says that, when he has more time, he would like to talk to Banquo about the witches: 'let us speak Our free hearts each to other' (*1*, 3, 153–4); *and*: 'when we can entreat an hour to serve, We would spend it in some words upon that business' (*2*, 1, 22–3). Devise two such scenes, showing how the relationship of the two men has changed between the first and second of the scenes.

C5 Give full TV coverage for the murder of Duncan—don't forget to interview the Porter and the Old Man, and to check the weather reports for that night. If possible, arrange that there should be signing for deaf people.

C6 Critics think that *Act 3*, Scene 5 was not written by Shakespeare; replace it with a new scene for the witches.

C7 Young Siward dies fighting for his country's freedom. Interview his father on a TV programme called 'Alas, poor country' (*4*, 3, 166).

C8 Bring the witches to court, and have them tried by a jury.

D Context Questions Questions like these, which are sometimes used in written examinations, can also be helpful as a class revision quiz, testing knowledge of the play and some understanding of its words.

D1   Do not muse at me, my most worthy friends.
I have a strange infirmity which is nothing
To those that know me. Come, love and health to all,
Then I'll sit down. Give me some wine; fill full!
I drink to th'general joy o'th'whole table.

  (i) Who is speaking, and on what occasion?
 (ii) What has caused him to behave strangely?
(iii) What happens immediately after these lines?

D2   Art thou afeard
To be the same in thine own act and valour,
As thou art in desire? Wouldst thou have that
Which thou esteem'st the ornament of life,
And live a coward in thine own esteem.

  (i) Who is speaking, and to whom?
 (ii) What is the person addressed afraid to do?
(iii) What effect does this speech have on the person addressed?

D3   Wisdom! to leave his wife, to leave his babes,
His mansion and his titles, in a place
From whence himself does fly? He loves us not,
He wants the natural touch.

  (i) Who is speaking, and to whom?
 (ii) What person is being spoken about?
(iii) What happens to the speaker shortly after these lines have
     been spoken?

D4   A heavy summons lies like lead upon me,
And yet I would not sleep: merciful powers!
Restrain in me the cursed thoughts that nature
Gives way to in repose. Give me my sword!

  (i) Who is the speaker? Who accompanies him?
 (ii) Why is he unwilling to sleep?
(iii) Why does he ask for his sword?

D5   Have you considered of my speeches? Know, that it was he, in
the times past, which held you so under fortune, which you
thought had been our innocent self.
  (i) Who is speaking? To whom does he speak?
 (ii) Who is the 'he' referred to?
(iii) What does the speaker want his hearers to do?

D6   Did he not straight
In pious rage the two delinquents tear,
That were the slaves of drink and thralls of sleep?
Was not that nobly done? Ay, and wisely too,
For 'twould have anger'd any heart alive
To hear the men deny't.

  (i) Who is speaking, and about whom?
  (ii) Who are the 'two delinquents'?
  (iii) What would they have denied?

D7   That which hath made them drunk, hath made me bold;
What hath quench'd them, hath given me fire. Hark, peace!
It was the owl that shriek'd, the fatal bellman
Which gives the stern'st good-night. He is about it.

  (i) Who is speaking?
  (ii) What is the speaker listening for?
  (iii) Who comes on to the stage after these lines? What has he
        done?

D8   We hear our bloody cousins are bestow'd
In England and in Ireland, not confessing
Their cruel parricide, filling their hearers
With strange invention. But of that tomorrow,
When therewithal we shall have cause of state
Craving us jointly.

  (i) Who is speaking, and to whom does he speak?
  (ii) Who are the 'bloody cousins'?
  (iii) Will the person addressed attend the meeting tomorrow?
        Why?

**E Critical
Appreciation**   These questions also present passages from the play and ask students to
comment on them; again you often have a choice of passages, but the
extracts are much longer than those presented as context questions.
Some examination boards allow candidates to take their copies of the
play into the examination room, asking them to re-read specified
sections of the play (such as those printed here) and answer questions
on them.

E1   *Act 1*, Scene 7, lines 47–59
Lady Macbeth

                              What beast was't then
That made you break this enterprise to me?
When you durst do it, then you were a man.
And to be more than what you were, you would
Be so much more the man. Nor time, nor place   5
Did then adhere, and yet you would make both.
They have made themselves, and that their fitness now
Does unmake you. I have given suck and know
How tender 'tis to love the babe that milks me:
I would, while it was smiling in my face,   10
Have pluck'd my nipple from his boneless gums,
And dash'd the brains out, had I so sworn
As you have done to this.

Making special reference to the above passage, discuss Lady Macbeth's understanding of her husband and her influence on him.

E2   *Act 4*, Scene 3, lines 114–131
Malcolm

                         Macduff, this noble passion,
Child of integrity, hath from my soul
Wip'd the black scruples, reconcil'd my thoughts
To thy good truth and honour. Devilish Macbeth
By many of these trains hath sought to win me   5
Into his power, and modest wisdom plucks me
From over-credulous haste; but God above
Deal between thee and me, for even now
I put myself to thy direction and
Unspeak mine own detraction, here abjure   10
The taints and blames I laid upon myself,
For strangers to my nature. I am yet
Unknown to woman, never was forsworn,
Scarcely have coveted what was mine own,
At no time broke my faith, would not betray   15
The devil to his fellow, and delight
No less in truth than life. My first false speaking
Was this upon myself.

Malcolm seems to have few *positive* characteristics, but Shakespeare develops him into the leader of the opposition: show how this is achieved.

E3   *Act 3*, Scene 1, lines 49–73

Macbeth

                    To be thus is nothing,
But to be safely thus. Our fears in Banquo
Stick deep, and in his royalty of nature
Reigns that which would be fear'd. 'Tis much he dares,
And to that dauntless temper of his mind,   5
He hath a wisdom that doth guide his valour
To act in safety. There is none but he
Whose being I do fear; and under him
My genius is rebuk'd, as, it is said,
Mark Antony's was by Caesar. He chid the sisters   10
When first they put the name of king upon me
And bade them speak to him. Then prophet-like,
They hail'd him father to a line of kings.
Upon my head they plac'd a fruitless crown,
And put a barren sceptre in my gripe,   15
Thence to be wrench'd with an unlineal hand,
No son of mine succeeding. If't be so,
For Banquo's issue have I fil'd my mind;
For them, the gracious Duncan have I murder'd;
Put rancours in the vessel of my peace   20
Only for them, and mine eternal jewel
Given to the common enemy of man,
To make them kings, the seeds of Banquo kings.
Rather than so, come fate into the lists,
And champion me to th'utterance.

With the help of this passage, attempt to analyse the complexities and confusions of Macbeth's mind.

F Essays   These will usually give you a specific topic to discuss, or perhaps a question that must be answered, in writing, *with a reasoned argument.* They *never* want you to tell the story of the play—so don't! Your examiner—or teacher—has read the play, and does not need to be reminded of it. Relevant quotations will always help you to make your points more strongly.

F1   How important is the influence of Lady Macbeth on her husband?

F2   What have you learned from *Macbeth* about the Elizabethan concept of the king?

F3   Describe the character of Macduff, and show how Shakespeare wins respect and approval for him.

F4   Give an account of the part played by the supernatural in *Macbeth*.

F5   We will establish our estate upon
Our eldest, Malcolm.

Explain why this is an important announcement.

F6   Compare and contrast Lady Macbeth and Lady Macduff.

F7   What means does Shakespeare use to create 'atmosphere' in *Macbeth*?

F8   At the beginning of the play Macbeth writes to his wife as 'my dearest partner of greatness'. How does their relationship change during the play?

F9   Give an account of the function of Ross in the play.

F10   Describe how Duncan rewards good and bad service.

F11   Discuss the importance of sleep in *Macbeth*.

F12   Is there any comedy in *Macbeth*? Is it necessary?

F13   'Everyone in the play either suspects, or is himself suspected.' Show how true this is.

F14   Do you feel any pity for Macbeth's 'fiend-like queen'?

G Projects   In some schools, students are asked to do more 'free-ranging' work, which takes them outside the text—but which should always be relevant to the play. Such Projects may demand skills other than reading and writing: design and artwork, for instance, may be involved. Sometimes a 'portfolio' of work is assembled over a considerable period of time; and this can be presented to the examiner as part of the student's work for assessment.

The availability of resources will, obviously, do much to determine the nature of the Projects; but this is something that only the local teachers will understand. However, there is always help to be found in libraries, museums, and art galleries.

Suggestions　　**G1**　Witches and witchcraft.

G2　Staging the play: set and costume designs for some part of *Macbeth*.

G3　'the golden round' (1, 5, 27): the magic of the crown.

G4　James VI and I.

G5　The sources of *Macbeth*.

G6　Great Actors and Actresses in *Macbeth*.

Background

England c. 1606

When Shakespeare was writing *Macbeth*, most people believed that the sun went round the earth. They were taught that this was a divinely ordered scheme of things, and that—in England—God had instituted a Church and ordained a Monarchy for the right government of the land and the populace.

'The past is a foreign country; they do things differently there.'

L. P. Hartley

Government For most of Shakespeare's life, the reigning monarch of England was Queen Elizabeth I; when she died, she was succeeded by King James I. He was also king of Scotland (James VI), and the two kingdoms were united in 1603 by his accession to the English throne. With his counsellors and ministers, James governed the nation (population less than six million) from London, although not more than half a million people inhabited the capital city. In the rest of the country, law and order were maintained by the land-owners and enforced by their deputies. It was a period of high inflation, when political and social unease presented constant threats to the king and the establishment, and when poverty was widespread. The average man had no vote—and his wife had no rights at all.

Religion At this time, England was a Christian country. All children were baptized, soon after they were born, into the Church of England; they were taught the essentials of the Christian faith, and instructed in their duty to God and to humankind.

Marriages were performed, and funerals conducted, only by the licensed clergy and in accordance with the Church's rites and ceremonies. Attendance at divine service was compulsory; absences (without good—medical—reason) could be punished by fines. By such means, the authorities were able to keep some check on the populace—recording births, marriages, and deaths; being alert to any religious nonconformity, which could be politically dangerous; and ensuring a minimum of orthodox instruction through the official 'Homilies' which were regularly preached from the pulpits of all parish churches throughout the realm.

Following Henry VIII's break away from the Church of Rome, all people in England were able to hear the church services *in their own language*. The Book of Common Prayer was used in every church, and an English translation of the Bible was read aloud in public. The Christian religion had never been so well taught before!

Education

School education reinforced the Church's teaching. From the age of four, boys might attend the 'petty school' (French '*petite école*') to learn the rudiments of reading and writing along with a few prayers; some schools also included work with numbers. At the age of seven, the boy was ready for the grammar school (if his father was willing and able to pay the fees). Here a thorough grounding in Latin grammar was followed by translation work and the study of Roman authors, paying attention as much to style as to matter. The arts of fine writing were thus inculcated from early youth.

A very few students proceeded to university; these were either clever scholarship boys, or else the sons of noblemen. Girls stayed at home, and acquired domestic and social skills—cooking, sewing, perhaps even music. The lucky ones might learn to read and write.

Language

At the start of the sixteenth century the English had a very poor opinion of their own language: there was little serious writing in English, and hardly any literature. Latin was the language of international scholarship, and Englishmen admired the eloquence of the Romans. They made many translations, and in this way they extended the resources of their own language, increasing its vocabulary and stretching its grammatical structures. French, Italian, and Spanish works were also translated and—for the first time—there were English versions of the Bible.

By the end of the century, English was a language to be proud of: it was rich in synonyms, capable of infinite variety and subtlety, and ready for all kinds of word-play—especially the *puns*, for which Shakespeare's English is renowned.

Drama

The great art-form of the Elizabethan and Jacobean age was its drama. The Elizabethans inherited a tradition of play-acting from the Middle Ages, and they reinforced this by reading and translating the Roman playwrights. At the beginning of the sixteenth century, plays were performed by groups of actors, all-male companies (boys acted the female roles) who travelled from town to town, setting up their stages in open places (such as inn-yards) or, with the permission of the owner, in the hall of some noble house. The touring companies continued, in the provinces, into the seventeenth century; but in London, in 1576, a new building was erected for the performance of plays. This was the Theatre, the first purpose-built playhouse in England. Other playhouses followed, (including Shakespeare's own theatre, the Globe) and the English drama reached new heights of eloquence.

There were those who disapproved, of course. The theatres, which brought large crowds together, could encourage the spread of disease—and dangerous ideas. During the summer, when the plague was at its worst, the playhouses were closed. A constant censorship was imposed, more or less severe at different times. The Puritan faction tried to close down the theatres, but—partly because there was royal favour for the drama, and partly because the buildings were outside the city limits—they did not succeed until 1642.

Theatre   From contemporary comments and sketches—most particularly a drawing by a Dutch visitor, Johannes de Witt—it is possible to form some idea of the typical Elizabethan playhouse for which most of Shakespeare's plays were written. Hexagonal in shape, it had three roofed galleries encircling an open courtyard. The plain, high stage projected into the yard, where it was surrounded by the audience of standing 'groundlings'. At the back were two doors for the actors' entrances and exits; and above these doors was a balcony—useful for a musicians' gallery or for the acting of scenes *above*. Over the stage was a thatched roof, supported on two pillars, forming a canopy—which seems to have been painted with the sun, moon, and stars for the 'heavens'.

Underneath was space (concealed by curtaining) which could be used by characters ascending and descending through a trap-door in the stage. Costumes and properties were kept backstage, in the 'tiring house'. The actors dressed lavishly, often wearing the secondhand clothes bestowed by rich patrons. Stage properties were important for defining a location, but the dramatist's own words were needed to explain the time of day, since all performances took place in the early afternoon.

A replica of Shakespeare's own theatre, the Globe, has been built in London, and stands in Southwark, almost exactly on the Bankside site of the original.

Shakespeare's Globe, Southwark, London, England. Photograph by Richard Kalina.

Selected Further Reading

Editions: Excellent introductions to *Macbeth* are to be found in:

Braunmuller, A. R., *Macbeth* (New Cambridge Shakespeare, 1997).
Muir, Kenneth, *Macbeth* (Arden Shakespeare, London, 1951).

Critical Works: There are useful chapters, or essays, on *Macbeth* in the following books:

Bayley, John, *Shakespeare and Tragedy* (London, 1981).
Bradley, A. C., *Shakespearean Tragedy* (London, 1904; reprinted 1978).
Brown, J. R. (ed.), *Focus on 'Macbeth'* (London, 1982).
Holloway, John, *The Story of the Night* (London, 1961).
Honigmann, E. A. J., *Shakespeare: Seven Tragedies* (London, 1976).
Knight, G. Wilson, *The Imperial Theme* (London, 1931).
Knights, L. C., *Explorations* (Cambridge, 1933).
Muir, Kenneth, and Edwards, Philip, *Aspects of 'Macbeth'* (London, 1977).
Sinfield, Alan (ed.), *'Macbeth': New Casebooks* (London, 1992).

Sources: Muir, Kenneth, *The Sources of Shakespeare's Plays* (London, 1977).

Additional background reading:
Bate, Jonathan, *The Genius of Shakespeare* (Picador [Macmillan], 1997).
Blake, N. F., *Shakespeare's Language: an Introduction* (London, 1983).
Gibson, Rex, *Shakespeare's Language* (Cambridge, 1997).
Honan, Park, *Shakespeare: A Life* (Oxford, 1998).
Muir, K., and Schoenbaum, S., *A New Companion to Shakespeare Studies* (Cambridge, 1971).
Langley, Andrew, *Shakespeare's Theatre* (Oxford, 1999).
Thomson, Peter, *Shakespeare's Theatre* (London, 1983).

William Shakespeare, 1564–1616

Elizabeth I was Queen of England when Shakespeare was born in 1564. He was the son of a tradesman who made and sold gloves in the small town of Stratford-upon-Avon, and he was educated at the grammar school in that town. Shakespeare did not go to university when he left school, but worked, perhaps, in his father's business. When he was eighteen he married Anne Hathaway, who became the mother of his daughter, Susanna, in 1583, and of twins in 1585.

There is nothing exciting, or even unusual, in this story; and from 1585 until 1592 there are no documents that can tell us anything at all about Shakespeare. But we have learned that in 1592 he was known in London, and that he had become both an actor and a playwright.

We do not know when Shakespeare wrote his first play, and indeed we are not sure of the order in which he wrote his works. If you look on page 127 at the list of his writings and their approximate dates, you will see how he started by writing plays on subjects taken from the history of England. No doubt this was partly because he was always an intensely patriotic man—but he was also a very shrewd business-man. He could see that the theatre audiences enjoyed being shown their own history, and it was certain that he would make a profit from this kind of drama.

The plays in the next group are mainly comedies, with romantic love-stories of young people who fall in love with one another, and at the end of the play marry and live happily ever after.

At the end of the sixteenth century the happiness disappears, and Shakespeare's plays become melancholy, bitter, and tragic. This change may have been caused by some sadness in the writer's life (one of his twins died in 1596). Shakespeare, however, was not the only writer whose works at this time were very serious. The whole of England was facing a crisis. Queen Elizabeth I was growing old. She was greatly loved, and the people were sad to think she must soon die; they were also afraid, for the queen had never married, and so there was no child to succeed her.

When James I came to the throne in 1603, Shakespeare continued to write serious drama—the great tragedies and the plays based on Roman history (such as *Julius Caesar*) for which he is most famous. Finally, before he retired from the theatre, he wrote another set of comedies. These all have the same theme: they tell of happiness which is lost, and then found again.

Shakespeare returned from London to Stratford, his home town. He was rich and successful, and he owned one of the biggest houses in the town. He died in 1616.

Shakespeare also wrote two long poems, and a collection of sonnets. The sonnets describe two love-affairs, but we do not know who the lovers were. Although there are many public documents concerned with his career as a writer and a business-man, Shakespeare has hidden his personal life from us. A nineteenth-century poet, Matthew Arnold, addressed Shakespeare in a poem, and wrote 'We ask and ask—Thou smilest, and art still'.

There is not even a trustworthy portrait of the world's greatest dramatist.

Approximate order of composition of Shakespeare's works

Period	Comedies	History plays	Tragedies	Poems
I	Comedy of Errors Taming of the Shrew	Henry VI, part 1 Henry VI, part 2	Titus Andronicus	
1594	Two Gentlemen of Verona Love's Labour's Lost	Henry VI, part 3 Richard III King John		Venus and Adonis Rape of Lucrece
II	Midsummer Night's Dream Merchant of Venice	Richard II Henry IV, part 1	Romeo and Juliet	
1599	Merry Wives of Windsor Much Ado About Nothing As You Like It	Henry IV, part 2 Henry V		Sonnets
III	Twelfth Night Troilus and Cressida		Julius Caesar Hamlet	
1608	Measure for Measure All's Well That Ends Well		Othello Timon of Athens King Lear Macbeth Antony and Cleopatra Coriolanus	
IV	Pericles Cymbeline			
1613	The Winter's Tale The Tempest	Henry VIII		